The International Library of Sociology

THE PROFESSIONAL TASK IN WELFARE PRACTICE

I0128932

Founded by KARL MANNHEIM

The International Library of Sociology

PUBLIC POLICY, WELFARE
AND SOCIAL WORK
In 18 Volumes

THE PROFESSIONAL TASK
IN WELFARE PRACTICE

by

PETER NOKES

Routledge
Taylor & Francis Group

LONDON AND NEW YORK

First published in 1967 by
Routledge

Reprinted in 1998, 2001 by
Routledge
2 Park Square, Milton Park, Abingdon, Oxon, OX14 4RN
Simultaneously published in the USA and Canada by Routledge
711 Third Avenue, New York, NY 10017
Transferred to Digital Printing 2007

Routledge is an imprint of the Taylor & Francis Group

Transferred to digital print 2013

The publishers have made every effort to contact authors/copyright holders
of the works reprinted in *The International Library of Sociology.*
This has not been possible in every case, however, and we would
welcome correspondence from those individuals/companies
we have been unable to trace.

British Library Cataloguing in Publication Data
A CIP catalogue record for this book
is available from the British Library

The Professional Task in Welfare Practice

ISBN 978-0-415-17720-7 (hbk)
ISBN 978-0-415-86375-9 (pbk)

Publisher's Note
The publisher has gone to great lengths to ensure the quality of this
reprint but points out that some imperfections in the original
may be apparent

Contents

Preface

This book is concerned with the nature of the professional task in such occupations as schoolteaching, mental hospital psychiatry and prison and borstal work. These occupations, and others, I refer to as the 'welfare professions'.

The welfare professions can be defined as those occupations where the declared purpose is to ameliorate the lives of other people, and to care for them, but where this purpose is accomplished by means that to the onlooker do not appear markedly different from those of ordinary social intercourse. These professions do not possess much in the way of a technology.[1] Surgery and medicine are therefore almost entirely excluded from this category, as although their declared purposes are those of the welfare professions their interventions typically take place via surgical operations and the administration of drugs. They can be included to the extent that the influence of intangibles ('ward atmosphere', 'morale') on a patient's career is acknowledged, as in psychosomatic medicine. Apart from this they do not come into the analysis. Psychiatry on the other hand is included in the category insofar as it uses varieties of psychotherapy, work therapy, milieu therapy and the like, but is excluded to the extent that it relies on drugs, chemotherapy, electroconvulsive therapy and similar resources. Occupations central to the category are the professions of education, including remedial and special education, and correctional work in prisons, borstals and approved schools.

The category of 'welfare profession' ought, on this basis to include all forms of social work. This is so. I have nevertheless focused discussion on those occupations that are conducted in an

---

[1] Technology: by this I mean literally *equipment*, i.e. the paraphernalia that are so conspicuous a feature of the working lives not only of physicians and surgeons but also scientists, engineers and air pilots. The choice of this as a defining characteristic of professional activity is not made casually. In the following chapters, especially II, III and VI, I hope to show that the presence or absence of a technology, in this sense, has a close bearing on other aspects of the professional role.

Preface

institutional setting such as a school, or a psychiatric hospital, or a borstal. One reason for this restriction is that the nature of the task in the one-to-one relationships of casework and individual psychotherapy is already the subject of an extensive literature, the most recent significant contribution being Professor Halmos's study of 'counselling'.[1] Little theoretical attention on the other hand has so far been directed to the difference that is made when a professional activity is conducted in an institutional setting. The term 'welfare professions' does not refer to the same group as Professor Halmos's 'counsellors' as I am concerned as much with the administrative as with the casework content of teaching a class of thirty children or running a borstal house of fifty boys.[2] It is not suggested that institutional work is of an ultimately different nature from work carried on outside an institution. It is rather that the practice of the welfare professions within an institution forces attention to aspects of professional activity that can otherwise be ignored, and in published discussion often are ignored, owing to the greater ease with which the demands of the social environment can themselves be ignored or otherwise discounted.

Thus the theme of the book as baldly stated in the first paragraph can already be clothed in some meaning. To explore the nature of the professional task in the welfare professions is to explore, among other things, the relationship between activities

[1] Paul Halmos, *The Faith of the Counsellors*, Constable, 1965.

[2] 'Administration' and 'casework': I am not referring merely to the distinction between administration and casework that is a focus of debate in social work agencies. This distinction is but one part of a wider sense in which I use both terms. Thus by casework I refer to the aspects of *individuation* in welfare practice: thus individual psychotherapy and the private tutorial are both casework settings in this sense. By administration I refer to those respects in which attention is directed to producing and maintaining conditions favourable to any declared task, including that of casework: maintaining order in a class and balancing a budget are both administrative activities in this sense. There is one respect in which these two aspects of the professional welfare role can be seen as ultimately fused: as in the socially oriented thinking that is central to the tradition of Utopian thought, a tradition that finds expression not only in the establishment of experimental Utopian communities but also most noticeably in the thinking of headmasters and others who have to administer 'miniature societies'. Many would suppose, however, that such a compromise eliminates the possibility of individuation altogether. This may be so in the extreme form that philosophies of individuation sometimes take. I nevertheless feel that such attempts to balance equally cogent considerations are more realistic than extreme philosophies of individuation, and on this account am inclined to see the immediate need to be the working out of a coherent philosophy of casework that gives due weight to the needs of the social system.

designed to supply the needs of individual clients, and activities designed to supply the needs of the organization and of the society within which the client's needs are met. What is the relationship between the casework and the administrative elements in school teaching, in borstal housemastering, in mental hospital psychiatry and in the custodial care of the offender? This question itself can be split into two. On the one hand we can ask what is the observed relationship between these considerations; to what extent are they in conflict, and when they are in conflict how are these conflicts resolved and decisions made? And on the other hand we can ask what is the proper relationship between them, i.e. what should be the strategy of the welfare professions?

The question: 'What is the nature of the task in the welfare professions?' has other dimensions too. It is, for example, posed by any examination of what we understand by the term 'treatment' in those organizations such as borstals and special schools that are not part of the medical world, where none of the distinctively medical forms of intervention are to be found, but where the term 'treatment' is in fact used to describe professional activity. What, in such settings, is the difference between a treatment relationship and a social relationship? How far is a 'treatment' relationship defined by the presence of a distinctive technology (as in surgery or medicine), and in the absence of such a technology what is the significance of the fact that we still define some varieties of social relationship as treatment relationships and others as not? What in turn does this tell us about preferred modes of social interaction? How far is the 'treatment' role sought because of the social distance it confers on the treatment giver, and how far is this an appropriate mode of social interaction in the welfare professions?

It is in connection with these problems that the question 'what is the nature of the task?' arises on courses of training. Students training to be assistant governors in the prison and borstal service, or to be teachers, or to be psychiatrists, have to arrive at some notion of what their chosen occupation is about, what their own contribution is to be and how they are to act. Are they to see themselves as adjusters, as behavioural engineers practising skills of a kind analogous to those of the surgeon? Graduate entrants to the prison and borstal services seem often to expect this kind of role and the role of doctors in society at large encourages perhaps most trainee psychiatrists to see themselves acting in this way. Or are they on the other hand engaged in an activity that is of a kind not essentially different from the conduct of ordinary social relationships except insofar as it is more conscious, and conceptualized in terms of a richer and more sophisticated theoretical framework? And if the latter then in what sense can they, ought they, need they regard themselves as 'professionals'? These problems (which occur to psychiatrists as well as to borstal housemasters and teachers) are real problems, they face everyone embarking on a career in the welfare professions, and it is the task of a training course to bring them into consciousness.

I have therefore tried to root discussion in the problems of the practitioner and the practitioner to be. My working life is spent in contact, not with undergraduate students of the social sciences who might be examining the worlds of penology and education as a preparation for a degree, but with people who are going to act as assistant governors, and teachers, and psychiatrists, and whose needs are therefore of an entirely different nature. My professional concerns are with problems of practice; so also are my theoretical interests. Hence the discussion is not of what the welfare professional ideally ought to be doing in some perfectly rational society – whatever that might mean – but of the task as it presents itself daily. The most easily overlooked question in any discussion of education, or correctional work, or even of psychiatry, is what the practitioner actually does, what is the significance of what he does, what he thinks he is doing and what is the significance of any myths he may create about what he is doing. These are the kinds of question the book sets out to explore.

I am aware that the term 'welfare profession' is clumsy and has unfortunate overtones, but so has every alternative I have been able to think of. In the early drafts the term 'humane professions' was used. In some ways this was better in that it acknowledged the humanitarian and religious origins of most pastoral work; 'pastoral professions' might have been chosen for the same reason. But one theme I want to explore is the attempts that are being made to break away from this tradition and to transform these occupations into something different. These occupations have not the technocratic, instrumental aura of surgery and medicine, but it might be argued that their future lies in just such a development. I do not believe this myself; I am inclined to see this hope as an illusion, and to relate it to a fear of and flight from human relationships that is the theme of later chapters. I prefer to think of education and correctional work as pastoral occupations, but the future is not at all clear, particularly in respect of the possible impact of technological and scientific development, and I am therefore obliged to use a more neutral term.

The text was virtually completed in its present form by the summer of 1966. The volume went to press in January 1967, by which time events had already rendered some of the detail out of date. Thus in the light of the spectacular series of escapes that occupied the prison service in the second half of 1966 the references in Chapter I to prison security have now a naïve appearance that they did not have at the time of writing. I found it impossible to keep revising the text in the light of latest developments and finally decided to leave these passages as they were. With regard to hospital planning, briefly referred to in Chapter I, new procedures issued by the Ministry of Health in September 1966 have clarified the relationship between site, operational policy and staffing discussed there. My use of the term 'operational policies' is now at variance with planning convention but this does not affect the argument as presented. The issue of task assignment versus patient assignment nursing seems likely to be submerged in the wider debate on 'progressive patient care', by which nursing staffing structure at ward level is varied according to the patient's stage of progress, to make the best use of scarce nursing resources. The whole question of the nursing profession's structure is now under review as a result of the report of the Salmon Committee in May 1966. These developments render somewhat dated the references to nursing organization without, however, affecting the points that they illustrate.

A great many people have helped me, at various times, to sort these ideas out. It would be quite impossible to acknowledge every separate debt of which I am conscious, and I can therefore mention by name only those who read and commented on the typescript. Marion Whyte, Barbara Weller and Donald Macmillan advised on social work, nursing and hospital planning. Such misrepresentations as remain on these topics are in no way due to them. To Norman Jepson and Nick Tyndall I am particularly indebted, not only for commenting from the standpoints of criminology and penology, but also for their unfailing courtesy when, over the past four years, I have questioned the basic premises of criminological thinking and remedial work.

Professor W. J. H. Sprott made suggestions for improving the structure of the book, which I have gladly adopted, and kindly pointed out an important factual error.

Chapters I and IV include material that first appeared in the journal *Human Relations*; Chapter VI is based on an article that first appeared in *The Prison Service Journal*. I gratefully acknowledge the permission of the editors to use these extracts.

It is customary on these occasions for the writer to acknowledge the invaluable help he has received from his wife. This, I have discovered, is no mere formality. The book is the outcome of a close collaboration over several years. To my wife therefore, for many things, but above all for listening, I dedicate it.

PETER NOKES

Leeds, January 1967

CHAPTER ONE

Objectives in the Welfare Professions

One way of beginning is presumably to ask what the welfare professional aims to *do*. What are his objectives? A number of
developments are forcing us to ask this question at the present
time.

One is the impact of management thinking on the welfare
world. Whether via 'management by objectives'[1] or via a search
for the 'Primary Task'[2] the effect is to force us to ask very
seriously just what it is that we are aiming at in our psychiatric
hospitals, in our prisons and in our schools.

Another is the increased attention being paid to training itself,
and the fact that the design and planning of training programmes
seems on the way to becoming a discipline in its own right. It
would seem fairly obvious (though the obvious is in this case
rather misleading) that some conclusion must be reached about
what students are being trained to do before a training course
can even be planned, let alone started. The practitioner may lose
sight of objectives in the minutiae of day to day practice – a
theme I shall return to – but it seems reasonable to suppose that
the trainer must confront this question daily if he is doing his
job properly. There is a certain amount of truth in this.

A third development, also one that faces the trainer, is the pace
of social change that has blurred the outlines of so many traditional occupations and introduced so many new ones unable
to provide their practitioners with any clear identity. Once pre-
liminary illusions have been dispelled students training to be
assistant governors in the prison and borstal service, for example,
want to know what their job entails. Students come on training

---

[1]Humble, 1965. [2]Rice, 1958, 1963. These two management themes are current in
the hospital service and in the prison and borstal service respectively.

I

courses for various reasons, but one is that they are looking for an occupational identity; they want to be something, to become something, to turn themselves from members of the class Student into members of the class Professional Person. Their expectations about how this is to be achieved are various. I do not think any of them actually expect a magical change of status as a result of some act analogous to a laying-on of hands. Many of them, on the other hand, do expect to be given *esoteric knowledge,* and instruction in distinctive *skills* (I shall return to these in the next chapter). But one thing they all expect, and it is an entirely reasonable thing to expect by any standards, and this is a job specification: information if not about how to do their job then at least about what is the job that they are required to do. Unfortunately they rarely get even this.

In fact trainers are not at all clear in their own minds about what it is that the practitioner is to do. It is not after all true that decisions about professional objectives must be made before a training course can get off the ground. The students are sent along whether we have got the matter straight or not, and somehow other things always seem to take priority. This may be why it often seems on these courses that discussion about objectives is the main thing that is going on. This is not entirely because we, the trainers, do not know our jobs. For one thing possible objectives are so often mutually contradictory. Though one can think of a number of things that prison and borstal staffs might do with their clients—containing them, reforming them, educating them, 'treating' them—it is certain that we cannot do all these things equally effectively at the same time. How are we to train a man for freedom in conditions of captivity? The old paradox still needs an answer. Similarly, in administering a hospital, though outside comment assures us that hospitals exist first and foremost for the patient, there is often a very real conflict between securing the well-being of the organization and securing the well-being of each of the patients for whom the organization was set up. This is one reason why it is difficult to tell students exactly what they are supposed to aim at, one reason why the content of training in the welfare professions is perhaps rather different from what it is in more cut and dried areas as, for instance, engineering, work study or plumbing.

And yet, paradoxically, the literature of the welfare professions abounds with quite unequivocal statements of what they are supposed to be doing:

'The purposes of training and treatment of convicted prisoners shall be to establish in them the will to lead a good and useful life on discharge, and to fit them to do so.'[1]

Similarly:

'The aim of the modern schools is to provide a good all-round secondary education, not focused on the traditional subjects of the school curriculum, but developing out of the interests of the children. Through its appeal to their interests it will stimulate the ability to learn and will teach them to pursue quality in thought, expression, and craftsmanship.'[2]

Medicine has generated similar statements. The World Health Organization has defined Health (I assume the purpose of this organization to be the promotion of Health) as:

'A state of complete physical, mental and social well-being, and not merely the absence of disease or infirmity.'[3]

Now statements of this kind are very familiar in all the welfare professions. It is this kind of affirmation that gets made from platforms at speech days, prize givings and similar ritual occasions. This being the case how can it be said that objectives in the welfare professions are unclear? One reason is that it is very difficult to say exactly what the status of these declarations is. They have an air of immense respectability, and most of us have been conditioned into a habit of mental genuflection whenever the indications are that one of them is on the way. Nevertheless I doubt whether they can properly be considered to be professional objectives. They can be seen as exhortations; they can be seen as things to be kept in mind; they can be seen as *ideals*, as I shall suggest in the next chapter, with this proviso – that as guides to action they are in fact useless, for the following reasons:

---

[1] Number six of the Prison Rules, 1949. In 1964 the wording was changed: 'The purpose of the training and treatment of convicted prisoners shall be to encourage and assist them to lead a good and useful life'. This is now Rule One.

[2] *The New Secondary Education*, H.M.S.O. 1947.

[3] Constitution of the World Health Organization, New York, 1946.

Objectives in the Welfare Professions

Organizational objectives and decision making

In the first place it is not at all clear what generalized objectives of this kind imply in terms of action, and in fact on occasions when decisions have to be made they prove to have little or no influence on the situation. This is most conspicuously apparent in current planning of welfare provision.

One area in which objectives have become the focus of conscious analysis is the hospital service. When a hospital has to be planned there are three major areas in which decisions have to be made. There are decisions about layout: the size and shape of the physical environment, i.e. buildings, services, access and circulation. Then there are decisions about staffing: who is to be present, in what numbers and with what duties. But neither of these areas can be decided on apart from decisions about what the organization is *for*. This is not something that can be taken for granted. One organization cannot do a multitude of things equally effectively at the same time. A teaching hospital cannot provide an entirely effective medical care service as the selection of patients for the first purpose has nothing necessarily to do with local patterns of disease.[1] This does not mean that we cannot compromise, in fact in so far as patients treated in a teaching hospital *are* treated they obviously reduce the call on other medical care services. Compromise takes place; the point is that compromise in such cases is conscious, it is *known*. Nor is planning entirely a matter of compromise between conflicting objectives, for objectives themselves have to be considered against the limitations of building methods, site, staff, and money available. Priorities have to be established between potentially conflicting considerations. Again the point is that this is not done in any spirit of facile optimism that everything can be done equally well at the same time. The fact that only one consideration can take first place is recognized and admitted.

As a result one of the most interesting aspects of planning carried out at this level of consciousness is the question of where the first decision is to be made, and at this point one discovers a very interesting thing about organizational objectives. Common sense supposes that the first decision must always be in the area of objectives and operational policies, and that layout

[1]Graham, 1962, p. 68. See also Nokes, 1967, for a development of the present argument.

4

and staffing alike should spring from this, but this is by no means necessarily so. For against this it can be argued that objectives and operational policies can only be meaningfully decided in the light of what staff are actually going to be available, and what money and geography permit. Planning carried out at this level of consciousness requires that objectives be precisely stated, and precisely stated because only then is it possible to assess whether they are feasible. This takes us a long way from the vague generalities of the speech day platform.

It is worth considering one example of this process in detail. The problem of how best to deploy those junior members of staff who come into direct contact with the client is one that crops up both in hospitals and prisons, and it is interesting to compare how the two services are meeting it. Thus there are two main ways of organizing nursing staff. One is the familiar task assignment system in which each nurse performs a set routine for every patient before commencing a different routine. The other is patient-assignment nursing in which each nurse does everything for a small number of patients, generally about six. There are many reasons for preferring the second method. It fits in with the increased demand for personalized attention, and also permits the formation of satisfying social relationships which psychosomatic medicine sees as an important factor in recovery.[1] But such a method presupposes the actual availability of well-educated, resourceful nurses who can exercise the high degree of personal responsibility that such a system requires. And these may not be available; indeed we have been training nurses for the last hundred years *not* to take initiative in this way. So if patient assignment nursing needs well educated and resourceful junior staff then the difficulty of recruiting such people might be seen as an argument for not pursuing these particular objectives in the first place.

This raises the very interesting question of what we understand by a *constraint*. The point is that to a very considerable extent a constraint is whatever we accept as a constraint, and what considerations eventually acquire this status depends a good deal on

---

[1] Impetus on this side has increased with the studies of the hospitalization of children associated with the name of James Robertson. See Robertson, 1958. The argument of patient assignment versus task assignment (or job assignment) seems, however, likely to be submerged in the general discussion of 'progressive patient care', as I have suggested in the preface.

where the first decisions are made. So if we regard patient assignment nursing as a paramount consideration then the difficulty of recruiting suitable staff in the junior grades becomes an argument not for changing the policies but for exerting direct pressure on the salary and career structure of the nursing profession. Whichever outcome takes place is a measure of what considerations have priority in planning.

Here we have planning in an organization that has become highly conscious about objectives. Now at the moment the prison and borstal services are encountering almost exactly the same set of problems. Here too there is a great deal of interest in policies that bring the individual prison officer into much closer contact with a smaller number of men than has traditionally been the case. An early such attempt was the 'Norwich' scheme; much more to the fore at the present time are attempts to introduce such policies as Group Counselling programmes[1] into prisons and borstals. This change mirrors exactly the change from task assignment to patient assignment nursing, changes that involve quite considerable modifications of traditional roles and attitudes. One wonders then what changes in staff and salary structure are envisaged to meet this change in penal policy. Individualized treatment programmes of this kind require intelligent and resourceful people at basic grade level, but these are only to be got at a price. In fact intelligent and resourceful basic grade prison officers tend increasingly to seek promotion to assistant governor. If individualized treatment is meant to be taken seriously then radical changes are clearly implied in the staff and salary structure alike.

There are no signs that changes of this magnitude are envisaged in the prison and borstal services. One reason is no doubt that the Prison Department of the Home Office has to cope with a variety of pressures apart from those consequent on policy changes. Group counselling programmes undermine the traditional supervisory and communication functions of middle grade staff, principal officers and chief officers, and pressures to retain traditional promotion peaks are highly cogent. Here again there seems to be a need to decide whether new operational policies are going to exert pressure on recruitment and salary structures,

---

[1] A derivative of group psychotherapy developed in California by Dr Norman Fenton, and introduced into the British prison and borstal service in 1957–58.

or whether existing salary structures and recruitment policies are
to be seen as reasons for not introducing new objectives and
operational policies. Logically the prison department ought to be
doing one thing or the other; what it does seem to be doing is
to make purely nominal policy changes as a result of attempting
to work within constraints inherited from an older system.

Depressingly familiar in all the welfare professions is a state of
affairs in which what goes on is a compromise between what is
supposed to go on and what an inherited situation makes possible.
Objectives seem rarely to have the same cogency in planning
welfare provision that they seem to have elsewhere. One reason
for this is the relative infrequency with which *manifest disaster
criteria*[1] are encountered. Doctors are able to indulge in a practice
that is known in hospital planning as 'shroud waving', the habit
of pointing to the disasters that will ensue if they do not get their
own way. Few welfare practitioners can do this. Grammar school
teachers are perhaps an exception to the extent that getting
children through external examinations is prominent among their
objectives. In the correctional world and in the secondary modern
schools, on the other hand, the sheer weight of balancing considerations regularly brings about a situation in which objectives
play only a minor part in determining what happens.

The results of this situation are often visible in architectural
arrangements. The functionless open iron staircases at Grendon
Underwood psychiatric prison are a relic of Sir Joshua Jebb's
radial prisons imported into what purports to be an up-to-date
penal establishment without apparently a word being said in
protest. The bath taps at this same prison are arranged so that
they can be manipulated only by the officer in charge – another
feature of the old 'locals'. It is surely in an incomplete specification of what is supposed to go on, of what the place is *for* that we
must locate the reason for these anomalies. Architectural arrangements, moreover, sometimes reflect the weakness of the practitioner's negotiating position in relation to outside pressures. A
characteristic of many post-war schools is the large plate glass
window to every classroom. This feature seems to reflect partly
aesthetic, partly hygienic considerations.[2] But these classrooms

[1] See Chapter II, p. 20.
[2] Possibly also a theory of child development that sees maturation as the crucial
process. If the teacher is a gardener then it is clearly appropriate to place the young
plants in a greenhouse.

7

are difficult to teach in, not only because they are over-hot in summer but also because, particularly if they have been placed next to a football pitch, they make the problem of securing attention acute. Teachers are in fact in a weak bargaining position *vis-à-vis* architects and educationists, and this has no doubt something to do with the fact that there are no physical circumstances in which the performance of their activities becomes manifestly impossible. Teachers are expected to rise above difficult circumstances. In planning welfare provision human limitations rarely enter into the calculation: one simply assumes that every practitioner is of heroic stature. This practice is traceable to the strongly ethical and religious component in welfare practice and to the idea of the vocation, matters that are discussed in Chapter II.

Organizational objectives and morale

Another reason why the highly general statements of objectives that are customary at prize givings are inadequate is that they give the practitioner no *personal* guidance about what he is to do. The problem facing the practitioner is always one of action. It is, as our students are constantly reminding us, what he should do in a particular situation. Now either the situation is clear cut and familiar (the G.P. faced with a case of tonsillitis, the schoolmaster faced with a G.C.E. stream), or else it is novel and ambiguous. In the former case generalized objectives are redundant; in the latter they are too vague to be useful.

But it is the unpatterned situation, where guidance really is needed, that the welfare practitioner increasingly faces. If anything is a defining characteristic of the welfare professions it is that in secondary modern education, borstal work and social work situations are rarely cut and dried. The welfare professions are typically concerned with those human problems that are left after the precisely defined and identifiable problems have been removed to the instrumental atmosphere of the medical and surgical wards, or to those schools that define their objectives as simply to get children through examinations.

So the doctor specializing in the treatment of delinquency, or in psychiatry generally for that matter, is likely to find at least one criterion of sickness absent, the patient's complaints. This in turn deprives him of a traditional cue for action, the relief of stated

8

suffering. If he begins to speculate on the actual objectives he might pursue he finds, according to one writer, at least three possibilities (Brewster Smith, 1950). These are 'adjustment' to the social milieu, 'cognitive adequacy' or 'insight', and 'personal integration'. These alternative objectives, moreover, are not necessarily compatible. Brewster Smith suggests that adequate adjustment to a society may often be achieved only at the cost of defective integration, through internalizing conflicting values, or else it may demand distorted perceptions of the self or of the society to which adjustment is made. In these circumstances the medical man may well find the pursuit of 'complete physical, mental and social well-being' a trivial slogan that fails to cope with the realities of the therapeutic situation.

Secondary modern schoolteachers find themselves in a rather similar position. Faced with a school population that is (errors in selection apart) non-academic by definition, they are therefore deprived of a traditional reference point, the idea of scholarship. For them advice to provide 'a good all-round secondary education, not focused on the traditional subjects of the school curriculum, but developing out of the interests of the children' is not illuminating. Nor are such suggestions as that they should be aiming at 'character formation' or 'the development of the whole child'. Actually the teacher's dilemma is similar in detail to that of the psychiatrist, for teachers too are regularly faced by a choice between policies designed to fit the child into a particular niche in society and policies designed to develop the child's potentialities as an individual. In the day of the organization man it is becoming increasingly difficult to do both at once.

Again in correctional work the same choice appears. Historically the prison service seems to have been dedicated to the needs of society to the almost entire exclusion of those of the individual offender. At the present time, however, there are those, including some practitioners, who sometimes seem to be saying that it does not matter whether a man leaves prison only to recommence a life of crime so long as his subsequent career is not marked by acute interpersonal difficulties. The work of penal administrators would be that much easier if they were able to make a firm choice either way. The prison rules, however vague about means are fairly unequivocal about overall ends, indicating that the main concern is to enable the prisoner to live in society without having to take to crime. But the rules are not, in fact, the only pressures operating on the practitioner. From the same source, the prison department of the Home Office, comes the Committal Warrant, a document that says nothing about rehabilitation at all, but indicates that the task is to confine a prisoner until the expiration of his sentence.

The practitioner can legitimately complain, then, that the very generalized statements of purpose that are found in the welfare professions give him too little guidance about what it is that he is to do. He can also complain that because so little guidance is given he is rarely in a position to know whether what he did was done well. The welfare professions provide little in the way of *performance criteria* by which a practitioner can assess his own worth. There are two aspects to this. On the one hand the very absence of performance criteria may provide a high degree of job security, for if it is not clear when a man is performing adequately it is no clearer when he is doing otherwise. Teachers and psychiatrists are rarely sacked. On the other hand people do need to assess themselves in relation to some personal standard, as well as in relation to their colleagues, and this absence of intrinsic performance criteria may have something to do with the ritualism that is so common a feature of the welfare professions, the substitution for vague ideals of goals which, whether or not they have anything to do with the declared task, are at least measurable. Among these rituals may be mentioned the preoccupation with standards of bedmaking that is still found in some hospitals, an excessive concern to have the grounds kept tidy, and a tendency to rate people according to standards of dress or punctuality. Teaching throws up some prime examples of this sort of thing. I have heard a teacher declare publicly that the *first principle of education* was to see that there was an adequate flow of air in the classroom. I myself was told that if I kept a clean register and avoided trouble with parents I wouldn't go far wrong.

Ritualism may be wholly incorporated in the structure of organizational activities. The way in which in borstal establishments and secondary schools the whole of the organization's energies over quite prolonged periods may be harnessed to the holding of a sports day or a concert perhaps testifies more than anything to a need to have something to demonstrate. Adequate rationalizations can always be provided for these substitute goals:

school plays and visits abroad are, after all, legitimate aspects of education. The point is that they are peculiarly the aspects of education that are demonstrable to a not always admiring world. One suspects that at least part of their function is to provide means of rating performance in the professional group. 'My house won the football shield' is seen as a valid claim to professional effectiveness among many borstal housemasters. And to secure *promotion* in any organization it is necessary to be at least visible.

The roots of organizational ambiguity

What, then, are we to say about this? The lack of clear objectives affects planning and efficient functioning on the one hand, morale on the other. One possible attitude is simply that it has got to stop; the welfare professions must put their house in order. Now if we do say this, and many of us do, we make by implication an important assumption about social problems, that the trouble lies with people. We make this assumption whether the people we have in mind are the practitioners, who simply are not good enough (a commonly held view when discussion turns to teachers or prison staff), or whether we mean 'management', which is out of date (an increasingly popular argument), or whether we mean simply 'them'. But wherever we do locate the trouble the implication is that someone is at fault (or perhaps sick). Now at the present time welfare professionals are beginning to turn to management experts for help with their problems – certainly in the prison and hospital services, and there are signs that educationists are beginning to take an interest in management too – and the interesting thing is that the message of much management thinking seems to be on exactly similar lines. Management theorists are not contemplatives, they are activists. They are out to improve things, and the transition from contemplation to action is generally marked by making someone, somewhere, change his habits. Thus it is not unusual for commentators to describe the prison and hospital services as existing in a state of 'organized chaos' for want of clear objectives, and the clear implication is that something can be done about it. In fact claims that the first duty of any management is to identify the Primary Task, that improved management performance rests on the establishment of precise objectives, are in a very important respect *exhortatory* in nature.

Now I think this may very well be a useful way of approaching industrial and commercial organizations where, even in a genuinely competitive situation there is often a lot of slack to be taken up. To some extent the approach might also suit welfare organizations, for similar reasons. But I do not think it would go very far towards solving the problems of the welfare professions because I am inclined to think that the *situation* of the welfare professions is in certain significant respects different from the situation of industry and commerce. Specifically I am inclined to think that the chaotic picture presented by our welfare organizations may not be basically a management problem at all. It may be a political problem. It may be that practitioners are confused about their objectives because *society* is confused about what it wants them to do, and if this is the case the situation is not going to be mended by exhortation, or training, or therapy. In the case of prisons society wants custody and it wants 'treatment', and it wants both at the same time. Similarly it wants an effective system of patient care and it wants an effective system of medical and nursing education, and it wants the same organization to provide both. It is simply facile to suppose that in such a situation organizational goals can be resolved by taking thought, or by any therapeutic equivalent. Many people are now demanding that hospital activities be centred on the single task of patient-care ('after all, hospitals exist for the patients and not for the staff!'), and that prisons and borstals should become exclusively oriented towards 'treatment'. Such developments would certainly ease the practitioner's task by providing him with the job specification he asks for. The trouble is that the concern of outside commentators so often fastens on manifest deficiencies in single areas of an organization's activities without there being any apparent awareness that these stem from the need to do many things at the same time, each of which, as it ceases to be performed effectively, becomes a focus of public indignation. So, for example, as the prison service has adjusted itself to the demand for more therapeutic regimes effective security has declined, a matter that will certainly attract adverse comment in due course.[1]

There are, in fact, certain dangers in arguing directly from

[1] Written in Spring 1966. See Preface.

industrial and commercial situations, for notwithstanding the implied claim of many writers that all organizations are pretty much alike there is a sense in which psychiatric hospitals, borstals and secondary modern schools are markedly different from factories. Discussing industrial and commercial enterprises one writer (who does not make any extensive claims) states:

'The work of planning will include the establishment of the basic objectives of the business and any subsequent modifications of these objectives. The basic purpose will be to make and sell some article or service for which people are prepared to pay. This must be done under such conditions that the total long-term costs of operation are covered and a profit is earned sufficient to maintain the required level of investment in the activity. If these conditions are not satisfied the business, under a regime of private enterprise must ultimately disappear.' (Branton, 1960.)

It would be difficult to find any analogous necessary condition that secondary modern schools have to meet if they are to survive, at least any necessary condition that would be acceptable as an objective. Similarly when Dr. K. Rice says that the Primary Task of an organization is 'the task that an organization must perform to survive' (Rice, 1963) this is equivalent to saying either that mere survival is an adequate objective for borstals and similar places, or else that there are no bad borstals or secondary modern schools. Alternatively, to define the Primary Task of an organization as 'the task which it is created to perform' (Rice, 1958) is to ignore the extent to which original purposes may be rendered irrelevant by time, without there arising any pressing need to replace them by new ones. Non-commercial organizations are quite capable of surviving by virtue of the unacknowledged functions that render them useful to society, and it is therefore possible to assume a degree of conscious intent that may not be present, and that may be misleading even when it is. Organizations such as prisons, borstals, psychiatric and other long-stay hospitals and some kinds of school operate against a background of a fairly long history of never having had to do anything in particular other than contain people. The habit of thinking in terms of clear objectives and of precise means to secure them is not well entrenched partly because such a habit is not necessary for survival. Such organizations do not go out of business. Society needs custodial institutions in order to have difficult people out of the way. There is a sense in which it needs schools to keep children who cannot legally be employed off the streets. And it also needs to satisfy its own conscience that something has been done for the various categories of client, and once that has been done society does not need to enquire too closely into whether what is done is done effectively.

One might take the line, however, that the peculiarities of the setting ought not to be used as an excuse for 'inefficiency', that precise goals, though not strictly necessary, ought nonetheless to be set. In fact this is done. Psychiatric hospitals and penal establishments alike have become preoccupied with readmission rates in recent years; Professor Kathleen Jones quotes five quite precise criteria by which the effectiveness of mental hospitals may be measured.[1] There is nonetheless a sense in which this new concern with the measurement of effectiveness is *gratuitous*; the fact that measures, instead of being implicit in the situation have actually to be devised sufficiently indicates the distance from the situation of industry and commerce.

In the welfare professions, then, the ambiguity of organizational objectives stems at least partly from the ambiguity of the situation, and it may be that there is a limit to the extent to which this can be resolved. Similarly for job specifications. It is sometimes argued that no job should be filled without there being drawn up a detailed job specification. This, of course, is exactly what so many of our students seem to be asking for. And yet the student and management expert alike may be suffering from a kind of Happy Families fallacy, a belief that all jobs can be reduced to the sharp outlines of Mr. Bun the Baker and Mr. Law the Lawyer. Certainly the established professions (medicine, law, engineering) do provide much more in the way of job specifications; they also provide a sharply defined professional identity with a great deal of expressive symbolism (e.g. the white coat and stethoscope) which is something else our students feel the lack of. But they perhaps do this at the expense of meeting society's needs in an ever changing world. The newer professions, on the other hand, have regularly to acknowledge the pace of change if only because

---

[1] Average length of patient stay; admission rate over discharge rate for patient; discharged as 'recovered' or 'relieved'; admission rate over beddage; average costs relapse rate of discharged patients. (Report of W.H.O. 1953; see Jones, 1962; Jones and Sidebotham, 1962.)

their actual titles keep getting changed. The medical social workers have had two names in this century, the people who are now the mental welfare officers have had three. This is very unsettling for people who need to know where they are, but it does mean that they are in a position to meet changing social needs in a way that is not conspicuously the case in the securer worlds of medicine, the law and the universities.

There is in fact a conflict between the needs of society and the needs of the individual whose job it is to meet these needs. The welfare professions are not comforting to be in, which brings the discussion back to the student in training, because the energies of students are often directed towards a flight from the impossibility of the situation in which they find themselves. Not uncommonly one finds suggestions of broken faith. People come into prison work, for example, for all sorts of reasons, including the desire to be in some sense therapists. But when they find that the practice of 'treatment' in a custodial setting is such a vague and ill-defined business there is an understandable tendency to seek security in an earlier state of affairs when the goal was simply custody and people knew where they were. A goal of custody is highly measurable and involves clear performance criteria. A goal of treatment on the other hand is hardly measurable at all, and many staff who have survived from an earlier regime find the attendant strains difficult to support. It has already been pointed out how in the welfare professions operational practice tends, notwithstanding official policy changes, to reflect traditional goals. This makes the task of the trainer doubly difficult because in training a readily available escape from the ambiguities of the work situation is into the role of John Bull, the Plain Man, who denies that any of these 'ologies' have much to do with 'the real job'. Such people are difficult to catch, for it is all too easy to equate the 'real job' with what the job used to be, particularly when routines and attitudes are still largely structured around previous objectives. Rule One says nothing about custody, but when prisons were merely custodial one knew where one was. So on training courses at the Prison Staff College there sometimes takes place a duel of conflicting authorities, in which the man who needs to know where he is will cite the Committal Warrant as his ultimate authority. Assistant governors in training very soon hear, and will repeat with all the owlish assurance of those who think they have made an original discovery that 'you can't treat them if you haven't got them'. Sir Alexander Paterson's equally cogent argument that you cannot treat them unless you are prepared to run the risk of losing them is less often heard. This perhaps throws a more charitable light on the ritualism that has already been discussed. For such needs on the part of the staff are no doubt at work behind the tendency for secondary modern schools, notwithstanding the stated objectives of the 1944 Education Act that brought them into being, to seek external examinations such as the C.S.E., or else to develop G.C.E. streams and perhaps to define the whole achievement of a school in terms of a handful of fifth-year students (Taylor, 1963). The welfare professions may be exploratory occupations, yet the personal needs of the practitioner constantly force attention away from this essentially *adaptive* function.[1] Perhaps our best strategy is to try to attract into these occupations people who are able to tolerate anxiety, or else to provide a good deal more support that we do for those we are able to get. Certainly it seems possible than although the welfare professions are not comforting to be in, the peculiar vagueness of objectives that makes them so uncomfortable is perhaps not something to be got out of the way as soon as possible, because this may be an intrinsic feature of humanitarian activity. Whether this is so is what this book sets out to explore.

---

[1] On this point, and on the theme of organizational objectives, see Donnison and Chapman, 1965, pp. 27-29.

CHAPTER TWO

Profession and Vocation in Welfare Practice

It is necessary to discuss in some detail the use of the term 'profession'. Discussion of this matter brings out sharply the respects in which the situation of the trainer differs from that of the teacher of undergraduates. For while the subject of professionalism is an established concern of undergraduate sociology departments, the sociology of the professions is of more than academic interest to the trainer. His students are personally concerned in this question because one of the things they often want to know is in what sense they can claim to be professional people themselves. Professional occupations have high prestige, and the professional cachet is being claimed by an increasing number of occupations. Senior prison staff and hospital administrators are among this group. Teachers have always been preoccupied with their exact status in the community. It is easy to dismiss such preoccupations as puerile. No doubt they are. The fact remains that people do worry about these things, and no trainer can afford to ignore what his students are in fact worrying about.

For these reasons the approach of the trainer to the theme of professionalism must be rather different from that of the academic sociologist. This is a fairly well worked area of sociology, and one that has thrown up a good deal of analysis and discussion since the pioneering work of Carr-Saunders and Wilson (Carr-Saunders and Wilson, 1933). But because his requirements are different the trainer of professional people gains nothing by joining in abstract debates on the subject of what a profession is.[1]

[1] Thus H. L. Wilensky (1962) p. 9: 'It seems wise to begin by defining profession. What is the difference between hospital administrators and garbage collectors, doctors and plumbers, that makes us speak of one as professional and deny the label to the other? Both in the minds of the lay public and professional groups themselves the criteria of distinction seem to be two: (1) The job of the professional is *technical*.

He is eclectic with regard to existing theories, and must be, because he is concerned not in exercises of formal sociology but in pinpointing the actual preoccupations of the practitioner. There is obviously a sense in which one uses the term 'profession' to refer to almost any white-collar occupation. Students know this. The fact is that they often show signs of wanting something more. What they seem to want, what is at the back of their minds is best identified by not talking about professionalism at all, but by taking advantage of an idea of Max Weber's, so far neglected and talking about the *virtuoso* role (Weber, 1965). Weber used this term in connection with his study of the varieties of religious leadership. I feel, however, that this is an idea that can be taken further; particularly that it can usefully be introduced into the discussion of varieties of occupational activity.

As I shall use the term the virtuoso role is admirably depicted in James Thurber's short story *The Secret Life of Walter Mitty*. In this story Mitty imagines himself performing successively in the roles of Commander of a small but immensely powerful naval vessel, surgeon, greatest pistol shot in all the world, bomber pilot and spy. I am inclined to see this story as epitomizing the secret dreams and aspirations of all of us, dreams that may have something to do with our choice of occupations, or failing that with what we try to find in whatever occupation we do eventually find ourselves in. What seems to be expected by many students of the job they have chosen, is the kind of glamour that is accorded to the doctor, the scientist, the air pilot and the concert pianist, to mention only a few virtuoso occupations. It is about these, the virtuoso professionals, that films and television serials are made, and in the Walter Mitty-like half world we all inhabit from time to time it is with these immensely potent figures, and not with the teachers, house-fathers, air-traffic controllers and administrators that we identify ourselves.

What are the characteristics of the virtuoso situation?

Social distance. Firstly, and obviously, there is the social distance that separates the virtuoso from the non-virtuoso. The air pilot

(2) The professional man adheres to a set of *professional norms*. The degree to which an occupation fits the criteria is the degree of its professionalization.' Social scientists not uncommonly fall into the trap of adopting the categories of society as their own analytical categories, which obliges them to find rational bases for what may not be rational at all. This is due to the ambiguous viewpoint of social scientists, discussed at length in Chapter V: *The role of the social scientist in applied fields.*

operates against a background of ground staff, the surgeon against the theatre attendants, the concert pianist is backed by an orchestra whose task it is to follow his every action. Typically the virtuoso performer sets the pace. I mention this factor of social distance first, not because it is the most important aspect of the virtuoso situation, but because it is the one that is most obvious, and probably the one that is most attractive to those who would play a virtuoso role. It is perhaps the factor of social distance that lies behind the commonly expressed desire for formal qualifications, and for restricted admission to practice. But these alone do not make a virtuoso performer, and indeed the factor of social distance has to be seen against a background of other considerations, some of which are more important by far. To a very considerable extent social distance and restricted admission to practice have meaning only in the light of the total responsibility that is given the virtuoso performer, which itself must be seen against a known background of potential disaster that would result from unskilled practice. This matter is discussed in Chapter VI in connection with the nature of treatment activities.

Skills. A second attribute of the virtuoso role that commands attention is the presence of distinctive skills. The virtuoso performs via a distinctive know-how that is not general but is restricted to the professional group and is typically acquired in training. Again this is perhaps why the hopes of welfare professionals seem so often to centre on the training course itself as a means of providing them with the desired status. But these skills are typically expressed via a distinctive technology, and where such a technology (surgical equipment, aircraft controls) is absent it is rare that other aspects of the virtuoso role are present either. It might, of course, be argued that every occupation, including the welfare professions has its distinctive skills. Certainly we heard talk of case-work skills and administrative skills. But it is not entirely clear that such skills are in any acceptable sense esoteric, confined to the professional group. This matter is discussed at length in Chapter III.

Esoteric knowledge. Thirdly there is esoteric knowledge. Apart from the knowledge implied in the mastery of skills there are other kinds of knowledge, diagnostic in nature. Strictly this kind of knowledge comes first, for before the virtuoso can act he has obviously to engage in an exploratory activity of deciding what action is needed. Diagnostic knowledge of this kind is not confined to the clinician. It is found in the concert pianist and the air pilot as much as in the surgeon, and even the garage mechanic has it. He too can tell you what is wrong without your having to, even being able to, tell him. Now esoteric knowledge of this kind does play a considerable part in the training of welfare professionals. Certainly the welfare professions, even if they lack much in the way of distinctive techniques, have an extensive repertoire of sociological, psychological and psychoanalytic information to which the practitioner can appeal. But again this is vexed ground. For diagnostic knowledge without distinctive skills hardly serves to define the virtuoso role. More importantly the virtuoso performer is in an important sense *bound* by his specialist knowledge. He seeks above all for accurate information, and is not in a position to select or reject information in the light of criteria other than accuracy. This is by no means the situation in the welfare professions, a matter that is discussed in Chapters IV and V.

These three attributes, social distance, the presence of skills and esoteric knowledge, are the most immediately visible aspects of the virtuoso role. Perhaps more fundamental, however, is the attribute of *autonomy*, with which is coupled the right to set essentially limited objectives, which in turn can be understood only in the light of the presence of a genuine possibility of *things going manifestly wrong* if the virtuoso is not allowed to work under these conditions.

Autonomy. The virtuoso sets his own objectives. Moreover, these are of an essentially limited nature. What is meant by a limited objective is discussed in this chapter, but at this point it can be said that the virtuoso professional does not concern himself with the ultimate, with ideals, but with the possible. And he is in a position to do this because only he says what is to be done. This is what is meant by autonomy. But this in turn must be understood against the invariable presence in virtuoso activity of

A manifest disaster criterion or 'pay-off'.[1] Virtuoso intervention makes a difference and is seen to do so in a situation where

[1] von Neumann and Morgenstern, 1947.

making a difference *matters*. Intervention must be seen to matter, i.e. non-intervention or inexpert intervention must be seen to bring in train some kind of disaster, for it is on his ability to ward off undesired outcomes that the position of the virtuoso largely rests. Thus the virtuoso concert pianist performs against a background of known possibilities such as playing wrong notes, forgetting the score, and so on, and his status as a virtuoso rests on the fact that these things do not happen to him. Similarly the surgeon performs in a situation where an incompetent performance could lead to loss of life, an air pilot in one where planes are known sometimes to crash. In general virtuoso activity must have a demonstrable outcome, and an outcome, moreover, that appears within a sufficiently short time for it to be apparent that it has been affected by virtuoso intervention. In the pure case there is a *critical act* by which events are seen to take a turn for the better – as in mending a fuse. This topic is resumed in Chapter VI in connection with treatment roles.

There is a case for saying that the presence or absence of measurable outcomes, or performance criteria of some kind, is the crucial test of virtuoso professionalism. It is this, for example, that determines the distinctive criteria of admission to practice in any occupation. Without a manifest disaster criterion, virtuoso status is not secured by the most stringent training requirements, nor even by a statutory monopoly, because there is no way of closing the door to the unqualified until the field becomes really crowded. This is why attempts to introduce mandatory training requirements into such fields as education and approved school housemastering are invariably abortive. Social science qualifications are stated as desirable in advertisements for housemasters' posts, but as a rule these are dispensed with. They are dispensed with because they can be, and because the job has got to be done by someone. Similarly in teaching there is little in the specifically educational activities of the teacher that can be shown to be the unique consequence of initial training and qualification.[1] (I am not here referring to such matters as the possession of an appropriate degree being a prerequisite for teaching modern languages

---

[1] I exclude from this statement infant teaching: a great deal of esoteric knowledge and not a little actual technology is involved in teaching children to read and number. Also, for analogous reasons, remedial and special education are excluded. On the impact of technology on the teaching profession see Chapter III.

or science.) Consequently teaching continues to admit a proportion of the totally 'unqualified'. Experienced teachers claim to be able to detect the results of inexpert handling, but in general, apart from the special case of examination results, outcomes are too long term to be demonstrable. Non-qualified performance in the welfare professions rarely ends in manifest disaster. This is no doubt why lay hospital administrators have so far found it impossible to restrict entry to the trained, notwithstanding the use of distinctive letters after the name or, more importantly, the fact that they have a quite long established professional institute. Training and expertise are alike purely formal in the absence of measurable outcomes, and whether these are present or not would seem to be beyond anyone's capacity to alter.

But not quite. The argument so far seems already to have defined the welfare professions as unable to give their practitioners the status of the virtuoso professional. But such a conclusion would overlook the extent to which the setting of any professional activity is subject to change. Consider, for example, the matter of techniques and skills. The welfare professions have at the moment little to show in the way of specialized techniques, but we have no grounds for supposing that this must continue to be the case. It might indeed be that the whole basis of welfare activity is likely to alter within the next few decades. The possibilities of this happening are explored in Chapter III. Supposing, however, it were concluded that the welfare professions are unlikely ever to be conducted on a basis much different from their present one, we could only reach that conclusion as a result of a much more detailed examination of what the basis of welfare practice is. And in this the model of the virtuoso professions might well prove useful to point up contrasts.

The idea of a vocation

To what extent, then, do the welfare professions measure up to the criteria of virtuoso professionalism? It is worth taking a second look at the theme of objectives, asking this time in what respects objectives in the welfare professions have the limited quality that is found in virtuoso activity, and secondly who decides what these objectives are to be. Now if it is characteristic of the virtuoso professional that he establishes objectives that are specific and limited, then it must be admitted that this is rarely the approach of welfare practice. A point touched on in the last chapter but not developed was the respect in which welfare practice seems to be conducted in response to moral rather than to pragmatic considerations. Occupations such as borstal house-mastering, probation work and even teaching have attributes that seem to imply a claim to more than instrumental status. These people do not in fact see themselves as mere adjusters or social engineers. Indeed their activities seem to be (at least in part) ends in themselves, testimonies to notions of what it is felt right to do, regardless of whether what is done is merely effective in some particular direction. And these testimonies have their source in the values of society at large, not in the decisions of the individual practitioner except insofar as he accurately mirrors the values of society. The instrumental component is not excluded, of course, but there is present a component difficult to define without using the language of theology. This might be called a sacramental component. It is the presence of this that leads to the common claim that teaching, or prison and borstal work are not 'just jobs'.

Our welfare services seem to have grown up in response to moral as much as to merely utilitarian considerations. Both for those who established them and for those who work in them these services have always been considered more than mere means to limited and precisely formulated ends: they have been expressions of moral values, of ideas of the Good. Hence they have always been required to meet two quite different sets of requirements, to meet the needs not only of those who receive benefit, but also of those who provide it. The birth of nursing as a profession in the nineteenth century is illustrative of this dual function, for this development is only half understood if it is seen merely as a response to a perceived need for improved nursing care. It was also a convenient expression of the ideal of service common to many well-to-do young ladies of the time. Notwithstanding Florence Nightingale's reservations about Catholic nursing orders,[1] the uniforms that were chosen, the terms of address and the hierarchical structure alike suggest an attempt to create a lay equivalent of the conventual life. (In respect of poverty,

[1] ' "Excellent self devoted women," wrote Miss Nightingale of certain nuns, "fit more for heaven than a hospital, they flit about like angels without hands among the patients and soothe their souls while they leave their bodies dirty and neglected." ' (Woodham-Smith, 1951.)

chastity and obedience the Benedictine Rule itself has been seen as applying to nurses, as, to a lesser but still identifiable extent, to teachers too. Certainly girls' schools have sometimes been conceived of as sisterhoods, women teachers being expected to remain unmarried and 'dedicated'.)

This goes some way to explaining the failure to set precise goals that was discussed in the last chapter. Precise goals are limited goals, and one of the main sources of difficulty in planning the welfare services is an actual resistance on the part of many practitioners to thinking pragmatically in terms of means and ends in relation to policy. There is commonly a strong feeling that in the welfare professions one is not doing that kind of job. For example a disclaimer of any intention to '*do* things to *people*' is one of the most regularly heard comments from new recruits to the governor grades of the prison and borstal services, people who at the same time are often expressing a desire to become 'real professionals'. The sacramental component also partly explains the variety of admission policy that is so common a feature of the welfare professions. In the virtuoso situation the right to practise rests on the possession of specialized knowledge and skills, and the test of competence is ultimately competent performance in a potentially emergency situation. But in the welfare professions the criteria are not so simple. Closely tied up with the notion that the welfare professions are not 'just jobs' is the idea of vocation. And this idea is both historically and etymologically a religious one. It is not long since prison 'welfare' and education alike were the province of the chaplain. At the Retreat, York, a high value was placed on the efficacy of religion in cases of mental disorder.[1] This background may partly explain the almost universal appearance of sacramental qualifications for practice. Fitness is typically fitness to serve, and this is often felt to be dependent less on any technical skills than on a state of being, or on external signs that are presumed to indicate such a state. This affects even professions that have become highly technologized Thus a recent case (1965) is that of the would-be nurse who was refused admission as a student at two London teaching hospitals on the grounds that she was not a Christian. Similar requirements are very commonly made of applicants for places at teacher training colleges. (It is interesting, though, that

[1] Jones, 1955, p. 61.

24

we do not make these requirements of medical students, nor of graduate entrants to university departments of education.) It is worth noting, in this connection, that a *headmaster's* role features frankly sacramental components in that he is required to preside daily at some form of religious service.

One notes similarly how often there is marked reaction of distaste to the introduction into the welfare professions of concepts of *efficiency*. It is usual to find practitioners justifying their work not in terms of any known degree of efficiency in the pursuit of a given goal, but in terms of the 'personal satisfactions' that accrue to those who give themselves in this way. It is in fact quite common to find practitioners unable to make even a conceptual distinction between personal satisfaction and objective success. A 'good day' therefore tends to be one on which the practitioner 'did a good day's work'. It is not necessarily a day on which some outstanding degree of objective 'good' was done.

It would be difficult to underestimate the importance in the history of the welfare professions of the idea of vocation, an idea that is diametrically opposed to professionalism of any kind, let alone virtuoso professionalism. This is certainly why the idea of precise and therefore limited goals is not regarded with favour. The virtuoso sets himself a limited task, which he decides on after a conscious calculation of possibilities. And such calculations will inevitably exclude otherwise desirable courses of action. Calculations of this kind are increasingly being made in medicine and surgery, particularly in respect of elderly patients. The cost of replacement surgery and such forms of treatment as renal dialysis are very high, so high that the Hippocratic ideal of never withholding treatment has to be balanced against economic possibility.[1] The humanitarian tradition, on the other hand, is opposed to all such calculations. Here aspirations are boundless. If we ask whether it is possible to set aspirations too high the answer will generally be no. The higher we aim, so the argument runs, the better, and the better because the better people we are

[1] Bernard Shaw saw this sixty years ago: 'My laboratory, my staff, and myself are working at full pressure. We are doing our utmost. The treatment is a new one. It takes time, means, and skill; and there is not enough for another case. Our ten cases are already chosen cases. Do you understand what I mean by chosen? . . . In every single one of those ten cases I have had to consider, not only whether the man could be saved, but whether he was worth saving. There were fifty cases to choose from; and forty had to be condemned to death.' (*The Doctor's Dilemma*, 1906.)

for aiming that high. Aims, then, refer not so much to the planning of feasible social provision as to the personal ethics of the practitioner. Now this too has a bearing on staff morale, a matter that was introduced in the last chapter. For where goals are set very high there is by definition all the more chance of failure; indeed aims seem to be highest in just those jobs where, because of the obduracy of the material, the prospects of measurable success must often be remote. Many people enter the welfare professions precisely because they offer, as the advertisements say, a challenge, because much will be demanded of those who take them on. Precisely because such people are admired for doing this it is generally considered somewhat bad form to focus too detached an eye on their efforts, and on their actual effectiveness. And this permits us to assume that the idealism that brought them into the work always lasts. Sometimes it does, sometimes it does not, and anyone who has much to do with such people as schoolteachers and social workers becomes aware that all may not be as well as we would like to think in those professions that rely heavily on the practitioner's youthful enthusiasm. Recruitment literature for the welfare professions tends often to be romantic to the point of actual misrepresentation. I have before me as I write an advertisement that appeared in several national newspapers during the autumn of 1965 by which the Department of Education and Science endeavoured to recruit graduates into the teaching profession. The advertisement measures fifteen inches by six. It shows, in the words of one commentator, 'a black-shirted boy in front of a complex molecular model which might be recognized by five per cent of recent graduates'. Also to the point, moreover, is the fact that the salary range quoted goes up to £3,850. This, of course, is a matter of cash that takes us some way from the present subject of high ideals and humanitarian endeavour. But it does illustrate the tradition of pious fraud in the welfare professions because, according to the same commentator, 'A headmaster of a Group 13 school (the very largest) would be earning £3,850 after three years. I have heard it said that there is at present one man who is in this position; certainly there cannot be very many.' (*Guardian,* 13th October 1965.)[1] As a result of recruiting

[1] On November 25th 1966 a report published by the National Union of Teachers cited the average weekly 'take-home' pay of teachers in various age groups as

literature such as this, and literature that habitually over-
states the possibilities of action, disappointment is not
uncommon among those who have given their lives to welfare
practice.

In the last chapter two reasons were suggested why the practitioner may reasonably object to vague and generalized goals. One
was that these do not tell him what to do, the other that they do
not give him any idea when he has done it. Here we have a third
possibility, that generalized objectives are in fact ideals, and so
typically expressed in absolute terms that provide the practitioner
with an almost certain guarantee of failure. Abstract definitions
and statements of objective are not after all without effect. 'A
good all-round education – developing out of the interests of the
child', 'A state of complete physical, mental and social well-
being' may have little actual bearing on the practitioner's daily
work. But to the extent that such slogans are taken seriously it is
clear that they involve the practitioner and his organization in a
form of inevitable inefficiency. If efficiency is defined as a relationship between objectives and achievements then inefficiency can
clearly result from setting objectives too high. Few social agencies
can live up to the high aspirations that many would set them. It
may be objected that this kind of inefficiency is admissible. The
Christian tradition requires us to give and not to count the cost.
The secular version of this philosophy is that if we do not aim
at a star we are unlikely to hit even a minor planet. This may be
true, though it seems to involve questionable assumptions about
the forces promoting the advancement of knowledge. It certainly
involves questionable assumptions about the limits of human
endurance. But in the welfare professions it has not been customary to plan for human limitations, and this too has had its
effect on practitioner morale. The ethical background of welfare
practice rests on a belief that with God's help all is possible, faith
alone can move mountains. Hence the ethical tradition is hostile
to planning, for planning becomes an impiety. Certainly it is
hostile to planning for human limitations: the assumption is

follows: teachers aged 20 to 24: £10; teachers aged 25 to 29: £15; teachers aged 30
to 34: just under £20. 36 per cent of all male teachers surveyed were obliged to
supplement their earnings by taking on extra work. Among male teachers with
dependent children the figure was 41 per cent. (Figures based on an enquiry among
1,200 teachers aged under 35. The enquiry achieved a 73 per cent response.)

always that we are all heroic figures. Hence the typical retort to the teacher who complains of the large plate glass window over-looking the football field: 'Any teacher worth her salt can hold the attention of a class, even when there is a football match going on.' And long after the specifically Christian basis of welfare practice has disappeared these attitudes survive in various secular philosophies. The welfare professions continue to draw heavily on the goodwill of their practitioners because of the prevalence of theories that seem to imply that people are infinitely flexible pro-vided you go about it the right way: theories that appear to stress the paramount importance of good human relations and the 'right approach' above all else. These have the convenient con-sequence that one never has to think about the nature of the organizational setting within which the practitioner works; more importantly that human limitations never need be budgeted for. The situation is masked by the fact that there is a lot of truth in all this, that the goodwill of staff has generally been forthcoming. But the result is to be seen in the many teachers who continue to battle with oversize classes in slum schools. The danger of the humanitarian tradition, the danger in the idea of vocation is that the human element becomes the area in which the slack is regularly taken up.[1]

Limited goals

Reflecting on these issues some writers have come to the con-clusion that we would do better to abandon the humanitarian tradition altogether and content ourselves with strictly limited objectives. The case for doing this is argued by Professor R. S. Peters in an interesting study of this problem in education. Thus while he readily agrees to a teacher, on being asked what he is aiming at replying 'getting at least six children through the eleven plus' he strongly objects to his replying 'the self-realization of the individual', 'character', 'wisdom', or 'citizenship' because:

'these very general aims are neither goals nor are they end products. Like "happiness" they are high-sounding ways of talking about

[1] C.f. Gerda Cohen on the theme of not being a nuisance: 'Nurses put up with bad equipment as just another test of their endurance, adjusting themselves to it, rather than flouting the hierarchy by asking for adjustment. . . . Tradition expects a nurse to laugh over stupid equipment, not to complain.' (Cohen, 1964.)

28

doing some things rather than others and doing them in a certain manner.' (Peters, 1959.)[1]

It does not seem beyond possibility that the borstal house-master and the probation officer might find similarly limited objectives suited to their own situations. And if it is objected that this would be to adopt too low a standard and to throw overboard the whole humanitarian ethic, then one can reply that the humanitarian ethic is only formally honoured anyway. The substitute goals mentioned in the last chapter (seeing the school play is a success, keeping the grounds tidy) *are* limited goals. What we must ensure is that the limited goals we inevitably choose are in some definable way going to benefit our clients. These need not necessarily take the form of concentrating on exam results or on success rates to the exclusion of everything else. More realistically and acceptably we might establish specific targets for each of our clients and aim at that. In fact we do this. Prison staffs do say such things as, 'We won't be able to stop this man returning to a life of crime but at least we can teach him a trade' (or teach him to read, or fix his teeth. I have the impression that inmates with obvious medical or educational deficiencies tend to be particularly welcome in borstals and training prisons). Come what may we do concern ourselves with quite limited objectives, and our only choice seems to be whether or not we are going to acknowledge what we are doing.

Yet this is to beg the question of whether it is entirely in the practitioner's hands to set his own goals, and so to the crucial issue of autonomy. For to make the assumption that he can set his own goals is to ignore the extent to which the very general

---

[1] C.f. also H. A. Simon's discussion of the place of ethics in decision-making: 'In order for an ethical proposition to be useful for rational decision-making, (a) the values taken as organizational objectives must be definite, so that their degree of realization in any situation can be assessed, and (b) it must be possible to form judgements as to the probability that particular actions will implement these objectives.' (Simon, 1945.)

C.f. also L. T. Wilkins: 'Operational research requires a clear statement of the problems to be investigated and the ends that it is desired to achieve. . . . If the administrator can state the ends desired, the work of the operational research team is to assess the likely outcome of a number of possible means towards the desired ends. Problems must be limited and specific and be oriented towards action – general solutions are not sought.' (Wilkins, 1962.)

If this is the case then a test of whether organizational objectives are clear is presumably whether or not it is possible to collaborate usefully with operational research workers.

goals that Professor Peters objects to yet have a function as affirmations of the values of society at large. And to substitute anything less for them might well involve the practitioner in a flat conflict with the rest of society.

This is clearly apparent in the educational field itself. The idea of child-centred education, which if it means anything at all surely means establishing limited objectives on the basis of a careful assessment of each child's needs, is, though formally honoured, in practice regularly subordinated to the idea of education as a matter of social justice, because it is social justice that educational theorists tend to be most concerned with. W. Taylor quotes Margaret Cole's comment on R. H. Tawney's *Secondary Education for All*: 'Even Tawney's eloquent plea . . . contains little more than its title suggests; it is a cry for justice for the deprived; it does not ask what kind of secondary education or what ends . . .' Mr. John Vaizey has added to this traditional concern with justice for the child a concern with education as a means of meeting future social needs. But he has nothing to say about the needs of children. The concept of Education with a capital E, has important egalitarian components that in fact may involve a total disregard of the needs of individual children. Thus the 1944 Education Act was egalitarian in provision and intent. Secondary education, which in the absence of any alternative model inevitably meant school and the classroom was seen as a privilege of which too many children had been deprived. This has effectively barred certain lines of development, however desirable they may have been from the standpoint of the children. Thus in secondary modern schools it has often been difficult to make any radical departure from strictly academic syllabuses without being charged with training hewers of wood and drawers of water. The result is that many non-academic children have been and continue to be subjected to regimes which have no relation to their needs and which may do them actual harm. Similarly any suggestion that education for adolescents might in certain cases take the form of supervised and guided experience in a non-school context has never seriously been mooted. The main recommendation of the Crowther Committee in 1959 (whose thirty members did not include a single classroom teacher) was that the minimum school leaving age be raised by a year. But the Committee made no concrete suggestions about what the fifteen-year-old group affected by this proposal might do during this extra year at school. It is not that a school regime cannot be found that would meet the needs of non-academic adolescents, though one regrets that thought should be necessarily confined to traditional solutions. It is that any serious attempt to meet individual needs in education is likely to fly in the face of what enlightened and liberal opinion thinks to be just. The main recommendation of the Crowther Committee, which was hailed by the liberal press as a triumph of democracy, was met by the teachers, if the correspondence columns of the *Times Educational Supplement* are anything to go by, with unqualified dismay. Interestingly enough, and this perhaps testifies to the extent that what we say matters more than what we do, this provision of the Crowther Report has still not, eight years later (January 1967), been implemented.

Similar things happen in the fields of health and welfare. Thus at the moment the trend of opinion is strongly against institutional provision. Professor Townsend's book *The Last Refuge*, a study of institutional provision for old people, effectively focused a general feeling of distaste for institutional settings, a distaste that has provoked a good deal of thinking on the possibilities of 'Community Care'. Yet a distaste for institutional provision can easily have the result of releasing into the community people who might just possibly have preferred to be merely happy where they were.[1] Preoccupation with the evils of institutional provision may occasionally disguise a basically punitive presumption that old people and psychiatric patients ought to be able to stand on their own feet as we have to do. Similar things are happening in the correctional field where the endless stream of petty offenders who get themselves back into prison within a few days of being released still does not force our attention to the fact that some of these offenders get themselves back there because they need to be looked after. Imprisonment, we argue, is an undesirable experi-

[1] Sullivan, approaching this problem from the standpoint not of a reformer but of someone with a lifetime's clinical experience, concluded that at least some aspects of hospitalization were beneficial to patients. Stanton and Schwartz quote his view that '. . . the severity of any mental disorder is to an important degree a result of insecurity about one's status. . . . This part of the problem would be solved by removing the patient to a society in which vertical mobility is not possible. Just this, in effect, is achieved by his admission to the custodial institution'. Similarly they refer to his feeling that 'the more or less rigidly enforced ordering of life by the clock' was rather beneficial than otherwise. (Stanton and Schwartz, 1954, p. 14.)

ence, therefore any man will be happier out than in. But this simply does not accord with the facts of any prison official's experience. Some inmates would gladly trade their rights to be free for the privilege of being looked after to the end of their days in some kind of hostel, and we need to be much clearer than we are about why we think they ought not to have this.

I began by asking whether the criterion of limited objectives that is characteristic of the virtuoso professional is found in the welfare professions. And it seems that at the level of stated policy objectives are anything but limited. Largely because of the ethical and expressive aspects of humanitarian activity objectives are large scale and general to the point of being grandiose. On this account it does not seem that the welfare professions can be counted as virtuoso occupations. At the level of day to day activity it seems that practitioners necessarily operate in terms of limited objectives that closely resemble those of the virtuoso professional. But there is a difference. Within the limits set by the formal statement of objectives, limits which, because of the very generality of these objectives may be very wide indeed, we may do all sorts of things. We may even accommodate the rigours of abstract thinking to the needs of the individual by such devices as defining elderly people as geriatric cases to ensure for them a degree of companionship, letting dull boys dig the garden and run errands and calling it education. We may do these things because no one is sufficiently interest in what we *do* to stop us. But the one thing we must not do is to say what we are doing. The practitioner in the welfare professions can never forget that he is a living embodiment of public sentiments and that these must not be outraged.

The lack of clear objectives puts the welfare professions at a disadvantage both in terms of the morale of their practitioners and in terms of the claims they are able to make in negotiation. But it is not clear that objectives, at least those objectives that are formally stated, could in fact be much more precise than they are because they have an irreducibly expressive quality as statements of society's values. The welfare professions are only partially instrumental, only partially means of bringing about particular results with particular classes of client. In recent years it has become customary to stress the extent to which the degree of discretion permitted to schoolteachers in England exceeds that found on the continent. Taylor stresses this point. This may be true. The point is that this is not where the crucial comparisons lie. Where people's vital interests are affected (I am not talking here about such matters as arranging time-tables) the amount of freedom of action society is ready to allow teachers is, by comparison with almost any other professional occupation, very slight indeed, as is apparent in the recent increase in pressure-group activity. Certainly these groups are appearing in the medical field too. But there are obvious respects in which the doctor can still claim to 'know best' and there is no prospect of getting round this because of the danger this would involve to ourselves. Not so in education. Here we are all experts.[1] Hence the student who expects to be performing as a virtuoso secondary modern school teacher (or borstal housemaster) is on this account at least likely to be disappointed.

[1] 'All occupations in the human relations field have only tenuous claims to exclusive competence. This results not only from their newness, uncertain standards, and the embryonic state of the social and psychological sciences on which they draw, but also from the fact that the types of problems dealt with are part of everyday living. The lay public cannot recognize the need for special competence in an area where everyone is "expert".' (Wilensky, 1962.)

CHAPTER THREE

Techniques and Skills in the Welfare Professions

The absence of limited objectives seems to imply that the welfare professional is unable to claim a virtuoso status. What, then, about the criterion of distinctive skills? Is there a distinctive expertise, an instrumental know-how that is peculiarly the property of the professional group, and which marks them off from the uninitiated?

The distinctive skills of the virtuoso professional are typically acquired in the course of training. Yet training in the welfare professions is relatively new, and not even yet entirely accepted as necessary. This suggests that specialist skills, if present at all, are not central to welfare practice. In fact the sacramental tradition has militated against training and skills alike, for two reasons. At its most explicit the tradition has seen training as exhibiting a lack of faith in divine provision. At a more humdrum level it might appear that training would jeopardize the spontaneity that is the essence of all genuinely social relationships. Hence the importance that has traditionally been attached to sacramental qualifications for entry, hence also the common preoccupation with personal qualities. This finds its most explicit statement in the prison and borstal service in the 'gold dust' theory of influence. Thus, we are all little bags of gold dust, and as we go through the world we influence our clients through contact, a little bit of the dust rubbing off here, a little bit there. Something of the same idea underlies the fairly long tradition in the teaching profession of supposing that teachers are born and not made. Among grammar school teachers of an old school stigma still attaches to training colleges precisely because they deal in the tricks of the trade, instead of turning out educated ladies and gentlemen who will exert influence by virtue of superior personal qualities.

At its best this tradition objects to the idea that one might deal with people instrumentally, or technically, seeing them as raw material to be processed. ('I don't want to *do* things to *people*.') And yet the least technocratic course of training must outrage this sentiment to some extent. There is an element of artifice in all art. Yet student teachers sometimes feel a reluctance to preparing their lessons in detail on the grounds that to do this destroys the element of spontaneity that is felt to be essential in all dealings with human beings. Newcomers to teaching are often disturbed by the element of play-acting that the least cynical experienced teacher will admit to. In training prison and borstal staffs there may similarly be encountered a resistance to learning how to interview. A feeling will be expressed that it is improper to teach this, and reference will be made to brainwashing and manipulation. Most difficult of all is the problem of teaching administration. The 'how to do it' of administration is in fact represented by the works of Professor Parkinson, Mr. Stephen Potter and Mr. Dale Carnegie, yet it would be impossible to introduce these works seriously into a training course. (It is useful to ask why not.) It is interesting that psychiatric training seems to be an exception to this rule. We feel no distaste for the idea that the mentally ill should both be expertly interviewed and also have things done to them. Harry Stack Sullivan has produced a textbook of 'how to do it' in psychiatry that would be outrageous were it written in terms of education or penology.[1] The fact that it is not, and that terms can yet easily be substituted, makes this book of immense value to any trainer of welfare professionals. But even this deals only with the face-to-face aspect of welfare practice. (Actually the technique of face-to-face relations is being brought into the open with the publication of books on social casework.) As far as the administrative aspects of welfare practice are concerned, however, (handling committees would be an example or dealing with problems of order) the 'how to do it' of education or penology or administration can still only be transferred informally, or via the specialized and publicly acceptable vehicle of the comic novel. It is interesting that on management courses for senior staffs of the hospital service this

[1] Sullivan, 1954.

35

kind of information gets disseminated not in lectures but at the bar.

Training in the welfare professions has of course not been encouraged by the fact that the welfare professions have never thrown up much in the way of an actual *technology*. 'Casework skills', when one encounters them, look much like somebody talking to somebody. Certainly none of the welfare professions has much in the way of mysterious equipment, or the various paraphernalia of the virtuoso. Yet the situation is circular, for one reason why these professions have not developed a technology is certainly the common resistance to dealing with people instrumentally. In point of fact teaching did develop something very like a most sophisticated technology, or at least a technocratic form of organization – the monitorial system[1] – at a time when medicine itself had scarcely extricated itself from the stage of magical activity. Yet this phase in educational history has been forgotten, and the names of Joseph Lancaster and Andrew Bell, who saw the invention as 'the Steam Engine of the Moral World' are not among those of the founding fathers of Education.

Whether by policy, or simply in deference to ultimate limitations of knowledge, the only type of influence that has been felt to be legitimate has been social contact, the kind of spiritual osmosis that is implied in the term 'personal qualities', or in the gold dust theory, and for which there can be no training. Hence

[1] 'In the Manchester Lancastrian School, connected with the British and Foreign School Society, he would have found over a thousand close-packed children, sitting on benches, all being taught together in one room, with only two masters and one mistress in charge. At first the noise would have been deafening, the crowd bewildering, but soon he would have noticed that there was order and system in the apparent chaos, that the multitude obeyed certain words and commands such as "sling hats", "clean slates," and acted as one child, that each nine or ten boys were in charge of another boy called a monitor, who taught them the lesson that he had lately learned himself, either summoning them to stand round him in one of the semi-circles marked in the passage at the end of the forms and teaching them to read from a board with the lesson printed large upon it, or else standing at the end of the form on which they were sitting and dictating to them words of the number of syllables suitable to their particular class. Dictation for the whole school was a triumph of organization. On the platform at one end sat the master, and at a signal from him, or from the "monitor-general," a sort of sergeant-major among children, the monitor of the highest class would lead off with his four-syllabled word, followed in turn by each monitor in the hierarchy down to the bottom. When the process had been repeated for six words, each monitor examined the slates of his charges and signalled to the master by means of a "telegraph" or signboard fixed at the end of the form; as soon as corrections were made, and all the telegraphs turned the right way, the master gave the signal again and another six words were dictated.'

(J. L. and Barbara Hammond, *The Bleak Age*.)

not only the difficulty of restricting practice to the qualified, for we are all capable of a social relationship, but also the absence of that social distance that is characteristic of the virtuoso role. History has no records of the outstandingly brilliant housemaster or child care officer, and is unlikely ever to have. Even where outstanding individuals like Thomas Arnold or Sir Alexander Paterson are thought of it is clear that their eminence rested not on expertise and esoteric knowledge, but on personal qualities, in fact on exactly those sacramental qualities that have been felt to be the main qualifications for practice.

Current developments

There are, however, signs of possible change. Developments in psychoanalytic theory, in experimental psychology and in bio-chemistry seem to be offering the welfare practitioner for the first time a variety of authentic techniques, and it is well worth considering what effect these are likely to have. In the British prison and borstal service, techniques of group counselling are already being used that have an obvious ancestry in group psychotherapy. More disturbing to accepted ideas is the sugges-tion that behaviour and aversion therapy might be a solution to certain forms of delinquent behaviour, notably sex offences and addictions (Eysenck, 1964). Also relevant to the correctional field seem to be the apparently effective resocialization techniques that are being used in the Chinese prison system, techniques that are perhaps closer to those of group counselling than we would at the moment be prepared to admit.[1] Most startling are the experi-ments in the voluntary castration of sex offenders.[2]

Moving into the field of psychiatry behaviour and aversion therapy again offer themselves, particularly in the treatment of phobias and compulsions, as also of such behavioural problems as alcoholism, drug addiction and sexual disorders. In psy-chiatry too possibilities of intervention now exist in the form of psychoactive drugs, E.C.T. and brain surgery, all possibilities that were not available twenty years ago.

Even education seems likely to have its technological revolu-tion. The teaching machine and the language laboratory are

[1] The literature of this subject is the literature of 'brainwashing'. (For a review see Biderman and Zimmer, 1961.)
[2] Craft, 1961, quoting Gibbens, 1951.

already familiar, devices designed to bring about a limited result with a high degree of efficacy. Less well known are the possibilities of sleep learning, by which routine matters such as the multiplication table can be learned whilst the child is asleep. This possibility, referred to by Aldous Huxley in his *Brave New World* (1932) has recently been given new prominence as a result of Russian experiments (Lustiberg, 1965), but has been practised in the United States for perhaps an equally long time, where the necessary equipment has been commercially available to students.[1] Finally even hypnosis has been tried in some Italian schools as an aid to routine learning (Associated Press Report, March 19th, 1963). Outside the realm of actual therapies, but sharing with them a strictly pragmatic approach to the problem of modifying behaviour in a welfare service context are to be considered the use of operational research methods in such fields as delinquency (Wilkins, 1962).

Now it is clear that these are techniques that would immeasurably add at least to the mystique of any profession that adopted them. There is no doubt, for example, that with the introduction of teaching machines into schools changes are implied for the teacher's role both within the school and in relation to society at large. For such a teacher will be one who knows all about the machine and about techniques of programming, as well as about learning processes (which until now there has been no guarantee that he knew anything about at all) and which will therefore mark him off as an 'expert'. Yet it is clear that the teaching machine and the language laboratory, far from being welcomed, are actually ignored by many teachers, occasionally even ridiculed. The only consequence of technological innovation at least in teaching, seemed until very recently to be renewed protestations that the scientific 'manipulation' of human beings will not do, with dark references to *Brave New World* and *1984*. An analogous situation exists in the world of sport. The aim of a football team is presumably to score goals, that of a climber to conquer mountains. But the use of hypnosis and benzedrine by football teams, and oxygen by Himalayan climbers has provoked exactly the same kind of moral debate.[2]

[1] Through the 'Sleep learning research association', Washington.

[2] 1966 saw two developments in the world of sport, the reception of which epitomizes the ambiguity of our attitudes to innovation. In October the use of 'walkie-talkie' radios by four overseas teams at the world angling championships at

In both these cases techniques are available that would enable practitioners to meet their stated objectives, but they are not welcomed. It is difficult to reconcile this fact with an aim of unqualified instrumentalism. Obviously the aim itself is not paramount: there are rules about how the aim is to be achieved.[1] Yet stated aims in the welfare professions say nothing about such limitations, in fact if their stated aims are to be taken seriously then welfare practitioners see themselves as pursuing entirely instrumental objectives, and certainly this would seem to be implied by the stated desire to become 'real professionals'. Teachers do admit as one of their objectives the provision of basic instruction in such subjects as mathematics. Rule Six of the prison service did say that the aim was to establish in convicted prisoners the will to lead a good and useful life. It may be that now we are offered precise means of achieving these objectives we are not so sure after all whether these are the objectives we wish to achieve. This may be why we changed the rule. But if this is so then we in the welfare professions are under an obligation to say so. For so long as we let it be understood that we are primarily interested in securing such things as effective instruction and personality change (for if it meant anything at all then this is what Rule Six meant) then we cannot be surprised if we are attacked for not getting on with it.

Great Yarmouth provoked Major Brian Halliday, president of the National Federation of Anglers, to declare himself 'sore and disgusted at the unsportsmanlike attitude of some of the competitors. . . . It was gamesmanship. They could pass helpful information to each other. . . . The rules do not exclude walkie-talkie radios, but that sort of thing was never thought of.' (*Guardian*, October 3rd, 1966). A month earlier, at the eighth European athletic championships in Budapest the elimination of the Rumanian world champion woman high jumper for refusing to attend the medical examination now required for the purpose of determining the sex of competitors forced attention in turn to the possibility that the performance of competitors from some countries might be being improved by biochemical means. 'Dianabol is a new drug which apparently retains proteins in the body and increases bulk and mass. The "heavy" men, the shot putters, hammer throwers, discus and decathlon athletes, now face the problem of whether they should take Dianabol. . . . Ron Pickering, the Welsh national coach and the best field events coach in Britain, says that he is at a crossroads. "Do I go on training my athletes knowing that they haven't got a chance against the Dianabol men, or do I give them Dianabol and alter their size and not be certain of the side-effects?" These side effects are reported to be a possible decrease in the size of the testicles and also some blood pressure trouble.' (*Observer*, September 4th, 1966).

[1] 'Every social group invariably couples its cultural objectves with regulations, rooted in the mores or institutions, of allowable procedures for moving towards these objectives.' (Merton, 1949, p. 133). See below, p. 45, footnote.

Such is the burden of repeated charges that the prison service, for example, should make itself more 'scientific', and use 'scientific methods'. Often these exhortations are entirely vacuous. The journal *New Society*, for example, reporting on Professor Sprott's presidential address to the Sociology section of the British Association in 1963 (*New Society*, September 5th, 1963, p. 5) says 'if we ignore retribution and act scientifically our penal system must change', but it is not made at all clear what the editors of *New Society* mean by the term 'scientifically'. Such appeals are easy to make. The fact remains that more informed opinion could make this charge a difficult one to answer by giving details of exactly what the teachers and prison administrators are not doing which they could be doing and ought to be doing if their stated objectives are meant to be taken seriously.

On the whole practitioners, while denying the truth of the charge that they are not doing their jobs properly, generally manage to give the impression of admitting the premise on which the charge is based, that theirs is a primarily instrumental activity. This is apparent from the lines of defence frequently adopted. Thus reassurance for the non-use of available techniques is regularly sought in the argument that what is not used would not work anyway, and conversely that what is considered permissible is also effective, if only in the long run. Aldous Huxley reassured himself about sleep learning by the argument that it worked only when harnessed to wicked ends. Similarly psychotherapists and penologists alike are prone to argue that behaviour therapy only 'transfers the symptoms', and that only long term psychotherapy or intensive casework can do anything about 'the underlying problem'. This may or may not be true, though one imagines that anyone who argues this way is in duty bound to demonstrate that long term psychotherapy and intensive casework even get as far as removing the symptoms. There is a suspicion here of an appeal to something like Adam Smith's *Hidden Hand*, by which the worlds of fact and obligation are so arranged that what we happen to approve is also effective. But this is a delusion. Mr. L. T. Wilkins writes:

'The many advances in the treatment of offenders that have taken place in the last century were, in the main, stimulated by humanitarian (ethical) considerations; the heart rather than the head has been the source of innovation in penal matters. There can, of course, be no objection to this. Indeed, if a case can be made for any change on humanitarian grounds it may override scientific considerations. On the other hand it must not be assumed that humanitarian grounds are scientific. The argument that because a thing is right it must also be profitable is not sound.' (Wilkins, 1962).

A similar retort might be made to those teachers who argue that teaching machines can never teach even elementary mathematics half as well as a real live teacher. This is probably self-deception.

Only at the very end of these debates does the real objection eventually emerge, that to deal with people by means such as this is somehow to deal with them improperly. It is here that the real force of the objection seems to lie, and it is curiously symptomatic of the present situation in the welfare professions that what would seem to be an entirely acceptable moral reservation should have to be presented until the very last moment in the guise of a spurious pragmatism. The ethical objection is a strong one, yet it is clear that to rely heavily on it is to define welfare practice in terms that makes it something quite different from the kind of instrumentally professional occupation that practitioners would sometimes claim it to be, and something that might not be so easy to defend.

The distaste, even fear with which attempts to deal with people *non-socially* are regarded seems to be very deep rooted. Such fears of 'brainwashing' seem to have refocused a suspicion of those who 'manipulate' that probably goes back to the days of the Sophist philosophers. Indeed with the publication of the works of Vance Packard and W. F. Whyte[1] this word has passed into very general use, providing the beginnings of a vocabulary that expresses anxieties extending into areas far beyond scientific advertising. There is, as already noted, a curious exception in the case of the mentally ill, for apart from a handful of politically aware psychiatrists (Zilboorg, 1948) it is generally thought proper that psychiatric treatment should involve the patient in 'having things done to him'. But we object to the idea that 'normal' people should be manipulated or brainwashed. Social relations appear to have a quality that comes not far short of the sacred; specifically we prefer to regard our dealings with others as though they were conducted exclusively on the plane of 'feeling', often

[1] See Bibliography.

in defiance of all evidence and even of common sense. The approbation we give to such terms as 'spontaneity' and 'sincerity' testifies to this attitude of mind.

Not surprisingly, then, if we examine which techniques are considered permissible and which not it becomes clear that approval is extended to those methods that deal with people at the level of conscious choice and denied to those that do not, and this regardless of questions of relative efficacy. So group counselling and social casework are admitted along with the traditional resources of argument, exhortation and personal example, not because they work (we might be less happy about them if we really thought they did) but because, whether they work or not, they do at least deal with people as social beings. (It is ironically the fact that they do this that may make it difficult for those encountering them for the first time to identify them as forms of 'treatment' at all.) And on the other hand behaviour therapy and the teaching machine tend to be rejected not because they do not work, for we can be pretty sure that they do, but because they do not acknowledge the need for people to deal with one another socially. In the last analysis there seems to be a claim that education that is not obtained in the course of social interaction is not worth having, that habit training and re-socialization that is not the outcome of conscious choice is a mockery. But if this is really what we think, we certainly need to become a good deal clearer about why we think it.

It is clear, in fact, that technical innovation and discovery can have the strange effect of making us much clearer about what we think we are up to in the welfare professions. Yet it would be unwise to predict the response of the welfare professions to a proffered technology. One cannot be entirely sure that the so far essentially social nature of philanthropic activity will make it impossible to assimilate such a technology. It might be that the appearance of a technology might put philanthropic activity on an entirely new footing. It could, after all, be argued that the welfare professions are only at the stage medicine was at a hundred years ago, a stage where one could diagnose and offer a prognosis, but in which there was little scope for controlled intervention. Medicine too at that time claimed the instrumental aim of relieving suffering. The point is that when, with the appearance of scientific medicine a technology finally did become available medicine demonstrated the sincerity of its professions by making use of it.[1] There is as yet little sign that either the correctional world or the educational world is going to welcome a similar technology, and one can only wonder whether the instrumental aim was claimed only because it was always possible to blame non-performance on the lack of suitable resources. To be suddenly presented with these resources is therefore to be made acutely aware that the claim to an instrumental objective was perhaps after all largely bluff. So if we claim that our objective is to teach children mathematics we are now required to explain why we are not using teaching machines generally to do it. It is not that no explanation can be made. But any valid explanation is likely to involve rephrasing our objectives as something rather different from teaching children mathematics. Similarly in penology we have been implying, for some time that our objective was to alter people's behaviour. If this is so then we are now required to explain why we do not use castration as at Hersted-vester and brainwashing as in China. And any explanation seems likely to involve an admission that when we defined our aim instrumentally we were merely seeking the approval of a society that is formally pragmatic and instrumental by defining our aims pragmatically and instrumentally, rather than in moral terms that would have been more difficult to defend or even to explain, and relying on fate never to require us to meet our obligations.

It is difficult to see how this dilemma is to be resolved. There are two components in welfare practice, the instrumental and the expressive, and a balance has to be struck between them. The highlighting of the social component helps to place in proper perspective the common assumption, for which practitioners themselves are partly to blame, that practice is exclusively instrumental in intent. It is on this assumption that casual comment bases the charge that the failure to use such devices as behaviour therapy can only be attributed to wilful stupidity. In fact the discovery that behaviour therapy changes the individual's behaviour brings us sharply up against the fact that this is not what we want, whatever we may have said in the past. And

---

[1] Though developments that permit the progress of a whole ward of patients to be monitored electronically from a central position are viewed with some reservations. 'Electronic pulse-recording, the summit of American efficiency, still sums up for the older S.R.N. all that is inhuman.' (Cohen, 1964.)

similarly the discovery that such measures as borstal training are not very 'effective' has the paradoxical effect of obliging us to admit that to some extent they are not meant to be 'effective' in quite this sense at all, but to do something rather different, perhaps even to testify to public notions of right and wrong. On the other hand it would be as foolish to stress the expressive at the expense of the instrumental as it is to do the opposite. For even if it is recognized that prisons and schools are not, after all, merely 'conversion processes' it is clear that they must be to some extent conversion processes. And it is certainly the case that the licence given to the practitioner by any acknowledgement that welfare organizations are not merely instrumental in intent can easily be abused. Remarks about human dignity and the liberty of the individual come out remarkably promptly on training courses as explanations of why we consider such techniques as brainwashing improper. Yet the consent of the individual has sometimes to be dispensed with in medicine, and in psychiatry things are done to and for a patient against his will. These things are done firstly because there are things that can be done, secondly because censure would be forthcoming if they were not done, and thirdly because on that account society gives particular people the responsibility for doing them. Only the first point applies to the welfare professions, and that only very recently. The second and third scarcely apply at all. At the present moment the practitioner is under little public pressure to be demonstrably effective, though Mr. Leslie Wilkins suggests that things are rather different in the United States.[1] It is therefore easy for him to misinterpret the peculiar freedom given him by his job as evidence of his own virtue. Occupations like prison and borstal work, perhaps also education, can too easily become a haven for dilettantes. If their stated objective is the instruction of children or the resocialization of adults then the teachers who refuse teaching machines and penologists who refuse aversion

---

[1] 'Treatment research cannot make use of the most usual tools of the scientific method; experimental designs are almost impossible to fit into the legal structure. Two or more different treatments cannot be allocated at random to a "control" and "experimental" groups, because to do so would not be seen as justice. There are notable exceptions to this in some other countries where the philosophy of treatment differs from that in England. In some American states, for example, public disapprobation is strongly expressed if treatment fails . . . but not if the sentence (by British standards) is regarded as either too lenient or toosevere.' (Wilkins, 1962).

44

therapy are guilty of insincerity. And whatever their stated objectives they could presumably be accused of cultivating their moral fastidiousness at the expense of their clients.

This is of course partly a matter of degree. A man may very well be allowed to withhold one or two possible resources on ethical grounds. But to withhold many is to raise doubts about whether one is genuinely engaged in practice at all. The time for exclusive non-instrumentalism is probably past; certainly there are signs that society will require more in the way of measurable efficiency of its welfare organizations. The only possible reply to the penologist who says that he does not want to do things to people is, now, that he seems to have got into the wrong job. Virtuoso professionalism is no longer entirely a matter of choice. It may be forced on us by technological development, forced, that is, if we continue to claim an instrumental objective. This in turn must inevitably bring about a situation in which the practitioner is in a position to set his own limited goals which, as we saw in the last chapter, he is rarely in a position to do at present. But it may be that some of us will want to abandon that claim; may even be that society decides that none of us must be allowed to make that claim, because the consequences of making claims in a situation where they can be put into practice has at last been appreciated. But, whichever way the decision goes, the appearance of authentic technologies and genuine possibilities of intervention will certainly force a decision on us all, and the reasons for that decision will have to be very conscious indeed. Thus one result of the appearance of a technology in the welfare professions is likely to be a rediscovery of the reality of moral choices.[1]

---

[1] With a consequent improvement in practitioner morale. In Merton's terms the 'anomie' of the welfare professions can be traced to the presence of culturally defined goals that are as limitless as monetary success, in a situation where the known efficacy of any procedure is enough to raise doubts about its propriety (Merton, 1949, pp. 131-160). Berne identifies this as a 'game' often played in social service organizations (Berne, 1966, pp. 147-150).

CHAPTER FOUR

Attitudes to Information in the Welfare Professions: the Themes of Reassurance and Faith

But the possibility of technical intervention is not the ultimate test of virtuoso professionalism. Many areas of medicine were until this century in a state where the practitioner could actually *do* very little that it was not open to an experienced mother and housewife to do equally well. Psychiatry was in this situation until very recently indeed: in the last century Kraepelin seems to have thought there was little one could actually do for a patient; diagnosis and prognosis were in his opinion the beginning and the end of the physician's skills (Stafford-Clark, 1952).

Nevertheless there *was* diagnosis and prognosis. One attribute of the virtuoso professional is the possession of esoteric knowledge, and while it is clear that ideally this knowledge ought to be instrumental, indicating what is to be done in a given situation, it must be minimally at least diagnostic, saying what is wrong. And it has already been pointed out that diagnostic and prognostic knowledge is, of course, available in the welfare professions; one might in fact say that it is in this direction rather than in that of treatment that most effort has been expended. Thus we may not do anything very scientific with our delinquents, our maladjusted children and our pupils, but at least we have a considerable body of sociological, psychological and psychoanalytic theory to explain why they are as they are. In this respect the welfare professions would seem to have as likely a claim to virtuoso status as did the nineteenth-century physician or the early-twentieth-century psychiatrist.

But the picture is not all that clear, for in the welfare professions attitudes to information are as ambiguous as attitudes to the more material resources that were discussed in the last chapter. One might suppose that professional practice in any sense of the word involved a recognition of the importance of accurate information, but this is by no means inevitably so. Customary ideas assure us that the search for truth is everyone's concern, yet in fact attitudes to truth, to *fact,* are highly ambiguous. There is, for example, a well established tradition that truth ought often to defer to charity. Few have expressed this belief more succinctly than Charles Dickens:

> 'There are some falsehoods, Tom, on which men mount, as on bright wings towards heaven. There are some truths, cold bitter taunting truths, wherein your worldly scholars are very apt and punctual, which bind men down to earth with leaden chains. Who would not rather have to fan him, in his dying hour, the lightest feather of a falsehood such as thine, than all the quills that have been plucked from the sharp porcupine, reproachful truth, since time began.'
>
> *(Martin Chuzzlewit*, Chapter 13.)

Similarly in *Hard Times* we find Bounderby's preoccupation with *facts* explicitly lampooned. (Were Gradgrind's pupils taught according to the Lancastrian method?) The author of an important recent study of *Dickens and Crime* (Collins, 1962) discusses Dickens' career as a reformer but makes no specific reference to this aspect of Dickens' habits of thought, yet Dickens perfectly expresses the attitude to information of the humanitarian, if indeed he did not personally determine the direction that 'progressive' thinking on penological matters took during the remainder of the nineteenth century, and continued to do in the present century. For it was Dickens who, through his *American Notes* (1842), brought about the modification of the Pennsylvania regime of separate cellular confinement, around which the model Prison of Pentonville was constructed. This highly articulate system,[1] a product of the same pragmatic ethic that produced the

[1] Fox, 1952; Howard, 1960. Solitude was the distinguishing feature of the Pennsylvania regime. In the prototype prison at Cherry Hill, Philadelphia, separate courtyards were provided to each cell, an arrangement reminiscent of a Carthusian monastery, entirely appropriate to a *penitentiary*. In the modified Pennsylvania regime introduced into Pentonville, prisoners wore masks whilst outside their cells. For a vivid account of this period see Charles Reade's novel *It's Never Too Late to Mend.*

Lancastrian schools, effectively confined, and seems also to have brought about personality changes. Unfortunately it also seems to have brought about a high incidence of insanity among inmates, a price that Dickens thought too high to pay for limited objectives and rational planning. (Later, in *David Copperfield* (1849) Dickens' objections to the Pentonville system as it had developed focused on the fact that inmates were better housed and fed than many a virtuous man outside. Inside every romantic radical there is an old Tory struggling to get out.)

Dickens' remarks to Tom Pinch illustrate the fact that in England the possession of the right sentiments has always, except for a short period when the Utilitarian philosophy held sway, attracted more approval than the ability to pursue a train of thought. Only once has England embraced for a time a purely instrumental approach to social provision and the Utilitarians or scientific radicals have never had an entirely good press since that time. Bentham, James Mill and Edwin Chadwick aroused the wrath of the popular radicals, of whom Dickens was one, and certainly there was something startling about a cast of mind that was able to formulate the principle of Less Eligibility, to say that the new workhouses must be uncomfortable or else people would prefer to remain unemployed. Yet it seems to have been the *saying* of this kind of thing that aroused popular anger. In practice the principle of less eligibility has always been and continues to be applied in such matters as the conduct of reception centres, as is suggested by the following comment from a newspaper that is not distinguished for tough-mindedness, but rather prides itself on being enlightened and progressive:

'Many of the hardships these families undergo are intended. However much they may not wish to, the L.C.C. are obliged to apply what is known as the built-in disincentive. Things can't be made too nice, otherwise the number of entries each week would increase, and families would stay here for ever.'
('Gaps in the Welfare State,' *Observer*, September 17th, 1961.)

But such candour is rare. Much more common is a situation where, whatever we actually do we are rather careful about what we say. This means that certain thoughts are inadmissible. Thus in the evaluation of policies around which many hopes gather a greater emphasis is commonly placed on aspirations than on

results. Correctional, educational and even psychiatric policies
tend to be evaluated according to whether they are 'on the right
lines' or 'point in the right direction', seldom according to
whether they are feasible, or whether they in fact *work*. Attempts
to ask such brutal questions are likely to meet with antagonism,
for precisely because welfare provision is so often thought of as a
battle against the forces of reaction and unenlightenment the
world soon becomes divided neatly into friends and enemies. So
the practitioner (and the social scientist, as I shall suggest in the
next chapter) is no longer able, because he is politically committed,
to maintain an entirely candid attitude to facts. One can distinguish two processes at work. One is the unacknowledged need
to be reassured that all is well. This need is inevitably con-
servative in results. It is the enemy of radical thinking, corrupting
the thinking of the most liberal and progressive when to be
liberal and progressive is merely to reflect received opinion. The
second is the pressure to be committed to programmes of reform,
to change things. Although this would seem to be an entirely
opposite process it leads to exactly similar forms of virtuous
misrepresentation.

Personal reassurance in welfare theory

The need to be reassured that all is well inevitably encourages the
denial of relevant information. A source of irritation, amusement
or despair, depending on how we choose to take it, to readers of
the *Guardian* have been the attempts since January 1964 of Mr.
Arthur Barton to discuss realistically some of the problems of
teaching in an urban secondary modern school, such matters as
the school leaving age and corporal punishment. Mr. Barton has
obviously little respect for educational theorists. He says such
things as this:

'Secondary modern teachers . . . are like front-line private soldiers.
We do not plan campaigns but only carry out orders. And in the
sphere of education the brass hats are infinitely more out of touch
than their military counterparts, who after all were once soldiers.

Most people who take a liberal and optimistic view of education
are not teachers of the 75 per cent of State-educated children in our
secondary modern schools. Much of the support for raising the

school-leaving age comes from secular idealists who look to education to do what was once expected of religion . . .'

(*Guardian*, January 23rd, 1964.)

This extract from a letter does no sort of justice to Mr. Barton's articles. His views are not 'liberal' or 'progressive' (in the special sense that these terms have in discussions of social service provision). He does not think the minimum school-leaving age should be raised to sixteen for all children; he thinks there may be a case for corporal punishment: with D. H. Lawrence he seems to believe that 'Love is in all generous impulse – even a good spanking'; he thinks the needs of the children need to be balanced against those of the teacher ('I have seen pathetic idealists . . . worn to the point of mental illness through their refusal to use conventional disciplinary methods. The cruelty of boys in the mass to a man who cannot or will not establish himself over them is terrible to see'); and he says that for those, like him, who are not preternaturally gifted 'teaching is a job to us, not a vocation'. Apart from an initial rhetorical remark: 'What subject provokes more well-meaning drivel?' (than Education), which is a claim I would be inclined to question, he argues his case sensibly and moderately.

His articles, during the two years they have been appearing, have inevitably provoked a good deal of correspondence, not all of it adverse. But the comments of one correspondent, the headmaster of a Quaker public school, deserve quoting. He began by suggesting that Mr. Barton 'has no doubt realized his immediate need to supplement his earnings from his efforts in the classroom' (an earlier correspondent, a professor of history, had also implied that Mr. Barton ought not to be writing articles at all) and goes on: 'Any teacher gets the discipline he allows – and deserves. If he is compelling interest in his subject . . . there is no question of discipline.' It was left to subsequent correspondents to point out the obvious fact (but in educational debate it is the obvious that never gets said) that 'conditions in a residential school for children drawn largely from the most idealistic and intelligent families in the country are not the same as those in an overcrowded secondary modern school in the slums of a great city'. The importance of what is being said here must not be underestimated. It amounts to a statement that it is just as possible in education as in nuclear physics for a commentator, through lack of relevant knowledge, to have no standing, and it further implies that in discussions of urban secondary modern schools liberal and mildly radical people in comfortable positions as professors and headmasters are almost certainly going to be in this category. This in turn is to question the indulgence that comfortably placed people permit themselves in discussions of the more gruelling areas of education, and for that matter correctional work, a matter that touches on the essentially aristocratic structure of power in the welfare professions which will be discussed in the final chapter.

The English tradition of liberal and enlightened comment rests, in fact, not on information at all, but on faith, in which the world of social service provision no doubt reflects its religious origins. (It is not irrelevant, however, that the cynic's definition of faith is the capacity to believe what you know to be untrue.) Faith is required in existing institutions, and if these institutions are the product of recent developments it is still faith that is required. Progressive comment commonly focuses on the difficulties that stand in the way of those who try to be objective about such venerable institutions as the monarchy, or the jury system. But this is not where the difficulty lies. The truth is that no difficulties whatsoever now stand in the way of anyone who wants to be objective about venerable institutions, while very great difficulties may stand in the way of anyone who wants to be objective about what is going on in our schools. This is why Mr. Barton finds it so difficult to get people to attend to what he has to say. He has not been alone, of course. The 1950s saw the publication of a good deal of adverse comment on the outcome of the 1944 Education Act, often in the form of what came to be known as the 'secondary modern shocker'. (Unwelcome information can be made palatable if it appears in the form of a comic novel, or otherwise in a way that enables it to be enjoyed and forgotten.) The reception these books had was interesting, for whilst they found considerable popularity among the public at large they were entirely neglected by educationists until well into the 1960s and in some cases were bitterly attacked by the teachers themselves. Michael Croft's book *Spare the Rod* (1954) described a not uncommon kind of bad secondary modern school, the kind of school that is still not so rare that it can be dismissed as an exceptional case. Yet the N.U.T. journal, *The Schoolmaster*, declared it was untrue or, if true, should not have been written. The N.A.S. journal, *The New Schoolmaster,* pronounced that its proper selling price would have been thirty pieces of silver.[1] In one of the few published comments on this class of book one writer comes to the predictable conclusion that most of the schools described in these books are unconvincing, and cites H. C. Dent's sample survey of 1956 that put the figure for schools doing definitely poor work at five per cent (Spolton, 1963). But even if no allowance is made for the inherent optimism of educational statistics the question still arises of whether five per cent is a reassuring figure, for to this one has presumably to add a larger figure to cover the schools doing mediocre and indifferent work. In fact, however, there is no longer any need to argue the point, for the climate of opinion has changed. With the general criticism of the eleven plus and the increased popularity of comprehensive forms of secondary education it is now perfectly acceptable to be critical of secondary modern schools. What is not permitted now is to ask whether the principles of social justice and optimum economic provision on which the comprehensive idea rests have anything to do with the needs of children.

The need for reassurance is not to be despised. The average teacher or approved school housemaster or youth club leader is convinced that he 'must be doing some good' because he cannot conceive of a world where his labours would remain entirely unrewarded. But in the hands of policy makers faith is dangerous for it leads to a suppression of information. In publications too one finds the most eminent professional people optimistically misrepresenting facts. It is revealing to study carefully the train of thought followed in part of Dr. Stafford-Clark's *Psychiatry Today,* a book that is obtainable in paperback form and probably represents for many teachers and social workers their entire source of information about the psychiatric scene. Dr. Stafford-Clark discusses the mental hospital movement of the last century. This was certainly the outcome of philanthropic endeavour and not of scientific discovery, a development in morals and not in medicine. Strictly speaking it was the outcome of a redefinition of a social problem. What had been seen as a disciplinary or a theological issue was now seen as a medical one. As a result the medical profession found itself called upon to deal with a problem

[1] Michael Croft, writing in the *Spectator*, June 4th 1961.

for which it possessed virtually no resources (exactly the same thing happened to the teachers in 1944), if it was to adopt any goal more ambitious than one of mere custody. The movement preceded by almost a hundred years the development of the first modern techniques of psychiatric therapy. (Phillippe Pinel unchained his patients at the Bicêtre Hospital in 1793, Sigmund Freud arrived at the Saltpetriere in 1885.) Yet virtually every reference made to the reforms of Pinel, Tuke and Rush represents them as advances in therapy. So Stafford-Clark says of Pinel:

'He was as enlightened in treatment as he was in abolishing restraint. He forbade blood letting, ducking, and every form of violence, and he introduced a moderation in the use of drugs which remains exemplary to this day.'

But these prohibitions seem to have been motivated by simple humanity and it is somewhat misleading to represent them as advances in therapy. Similarly in relation to Mesmerism Stafford-Clark says that it

'fulfilled an unquestionable need of the times. It was in fact the only available treatment for neuroses. . . . The work of Pinel and others was still essentially dedicated to the demonstrably insane, but the proportion of the population afflicted with mental illness outside the mental hospitals was probably not a great deal smaller than it is today.'

But this is the pure philosophy of Dr. Pangloss, and altogether too subtle. In this sense the rack and the bonfire fulfilled the same unquestionable need at an earlier date. Surely there is some question of whether Mesmerism was an *effective* form of therapy? And once again we see it implied that the work of Pinel and others within the mental hospitals was therapeutic in intention and effect.

It is not difficult to find reasons for this. In view of our sympathy with all forms of philanthropic endeavour it is difficult for us not to suppose that progress is being made all the time. Yet this, in the present instance, would be to attribute to Pinel and Tuke an objective that may not, in fact, have been theirs. There is nothing wrong with a policy of enlightened custodialism, especially when the lack of resources makes it practically impossible to adopt any other, indeed the acceptance in these conditions of a comparatively humble goal suggests a mature readiness to see facts for what they are. The actual state of nineteenth-century knowledge and the limits of therapeutic aspiration are suggested by Dr. Stafford-Clark's remarks on Kraepelin:

> 'He regarded the outcome of (mental) illness as essentially fixed. One type of illness would naturally recover. Another, equally naturally and inevitably, would have a progressively downward course. The whole process was subject to natural laws which, once understood, would give a key to prognosis and thereby provide the classification with an essentially practical bias.'

Kraepelin seems not in fact to have envisaged the possibility of therapy, and his sombre determinism is, understandably, little to modern taste. Dr. Stafford-Clark significantly feels obliged to relieve this impression:

> 'Kraepelin's attitude to therapy was not as passive as his deterministic attitude might suggest. Day to day management and care he regarded as most necessary. But as he based his system on the essentially unalterable nature of the diseases he described he was bound to maintain that the ultimate outcome would be unaffected, although their course might be modified.'

But 'day to day management and care' is not therapy in quite this sense. Dr. Clark is putting the best face on things, and there is nothing wrong about that. But there is no doubt that this optimism gives the non-specialist student a rather distorted picture of the facts.

Penal administrators are similarly served by criminologists and writers on penal matters. A passage written by Miss Winifred Elkin on the subject of probation deserves a detailed analysis. Again the passage is taken from a paperback that is widely read by non-specialists and by beginners in criminology and public administration. Miss Elkin is discussing the public image of probation:

> 'Ironically, the very fact that probation avoids removal to an institution makes it suspect in the eyes of many people. Because there is no obvious penalty or discomfort it is regarded as a mere "let off". But this view fails to grasp the essence of probation. It emphatically does not mean that the probation officer just lends a helping hand and has a few kindly words with the probationer. Every probation officer knows that nothing can be achieved if the probationers remain passive, and one of the primary aims is always the development of a sense of personal responsibility. Probation does not involve punishment, but it does demand effort.' (Elkin, 1957.)

This kind of statement is most familiar, and deserves very careful examination. In the first place it is clear that to demand effort of the probationer is not the same as to obtain it. This is not entirely a verbal quibble. One finds it difficult to believe both that probation officers are overworked, as Miss Elkin makes abundantly clear elsewhere, and also that probation invariably involves the degree of close supervision implied in this passage. The popular view may be substantially correct; certainly what Miss Elkin has to say by no means rules out the possibility.

Secondly people as a rule react to what we do and what we say, and not to what we *mean*. These are different things, and there is no simple relationship between them. So even if the public impression is incorrect it is not to the point to meet a criticism of what appears to be happening by a statement of aims. Probation may in fact always involve the probationer in a good deal of effort, but if this is so then it must be shown that it is so, and not that it is supposed to be.

But to argue that probation does demand effort is to shift ground on the central issue of whether the aims of probation are punitive or therapeutic. Miss Elkin appears to share the clinical outlook of most modern writers on the subject. She is therefore under no obligation to meet the complaint that probation involves no hardship by a statement that it does. It is precisely this uncertainty about aims that makes it so difficult to evaluate or even to understand so much of what is written on penal policy.

Miss Elkin has quite understandably tried to put things in the best light, but in doing so effectively obscures at least one crucial issue on the matter of probation. This is that if those responsible for the probation service accept as at all legitimate the concern of society, indeed the concern of *societies* as such, with public standards of conduct and morality then the probation service is clearly open to criticism. For to the extent that any substantial number of people believe that probation is a 'let off' then, whether they are correct in this impression or not justice has not been seen to be done, and this is a serious matter. If, on the other hand, court disposals are to be decided on exclusively clinical grounds then this is a possible position, but one that must not be defended by arguments that say, or appear to say, that 'treatment is a difficult process' or that it involves the treated in hardship or discomfort. Court disposals made on exclusively clinical grounds run counter to the principles of public justice, and there is no point in our deceiving ourselves about this, or in attempting to deceive society at large. A court disposal is not merely an administrative act. It is also a communication to the world at large, a statement about what the court thinks important, and what value it attaches to what other people think important. And it is this whether or not the members of that court intend to make a public statement, or whether or not they are even aware that they are making a public statement. For a statement is involved in the act itself, and this act will be interpreted by the world at large according to its particular notion of what the act is saying about the matter, in which the public is vitally interested, whether we like it or not, of reward and punishment.

P. M. W. Voelcker, in a study of the attitudes of parents whose children were brought before a juvenile court, notes that parents were more in favour of punishment than were the court personnel. More interestingly he shows that the majority of parents were under the impression that the motives behind court disposals were in fact punitive, and that the court disposed of cases according to a principle of graded or cumulative punishment. 'They give them a conditional discharge first, then probation, and then if they keep on, well, they have to send them away, don't they?' Thus court and public appear to possess two quite distinct codes in terms of which the same message has two quite different meanings. And this is a serious matter. For it is conceivable that while as a means of bringing the individual into treatment probation may be wholly effective, as a symbolic or normative measure, if this is how in fact it is being seen, it may be positively harmful.

Voelcker seems to be uneasily aware that there is a problem here, for he reassures us with the information that none of the parents he interviewed regarded probation as a 'let off'. But these were people with first-hand knowledge of probation. We need to know how probation was regarded by those friends of the children in court who had themselves no first-hand knowledge of it, and this we are not told. One feels in fact that the writer takes fright at this point. His train of thought has led him to an abyss, and he understandably steps back. And at this point he plays the trump card of every philanthropist in difficulties; he recommends 'increased understanding'. He suggests that 'the co-operation of the parent, of such importance in so many cases, might be increased if the magistrate could make even greater efforts to remove these misunderstandings'. It might, and then it might not. It is customary to maintain that increased understanding invariably leads to increased co-operation, but in this case one wonders whether with increased understanding co-operation might not disappear entirely. The problem is not that there is misunderstanding but that there is a genuine conflict of interests, which is only concealed by the fact that one side has a mistaken idea of what the other is about. (Voelcker, 1960.)

Faith is required in established institutions; faith is also required in individuals, and this too affects our attitudes to information. A frequently quoted remark of Winston Churchill's made when he was Home Secretary in 1910 (it appears as the motto of D. L. Howard's *The English Prisons* as well as at the entrance to the Officers' Training School, Leyhill) stresses the importance of 'Unfailing faith that there is a treasure, if you can only find it, in the heart of every man'.

Such a faith is manifested, for example, in the act of putting an old offender on probation. 'Let's give him a chance' is our attitude. Much of the impetus behind the opposition to preventive detention may well reside in the fact that preventive detention adopts a purely pragmatic attitude to the old offender. The charge that it in any case penalizes the wrong group – the compulsive petty offender rather than the professional criminal–is of course a realistic one. Yet there is perhaps also a feeling that it is improper to treat people statistically by making forecasts, however realistic these may be in the light of past experience, about the likelihood of an old offender going straight. Quite simply it acknowledges no possibility of divine intervention, and many people therefore feel that it is improper to place bets in quite this matter of fact manner. (Something of the same distaste is felt for predictions about the number of road deaths that will occur at Bank Holiday weekends.) Charles Reade's novel *It's Never Too Late to Mend* expressed in its title, as well as in its criticisms of the early Pentonville regime, the distaste of those brought up in the Christian tradition for purely pragmatic approaches to social problems.

Faith, similarly, is required of the teacher, sometimes in defiance of everything he knows about his pupils. The trouble is that faith merges imperceptibly into self-deception, and so into the deception of others, and so into a state of affairs where, for we cannot after all exist without at least some of our information being accurate, the effective working of society is materially encumbered. This comes out in the matter of testimonials and references. There are many teachers who would be most reluctant to provide information that was likely to lessen the chances of their protégés, even when such information was directly relevant to the matter in hand. As a result there are schools which are well known among employers and in the universities for the habit of representing every goose as a swan. Similar issues arise in connection with school promotions. In the sixth forms of most grammar schools are to be found one or two pupils who barely managed to scrape a couple of O levels the previous summer, and who will certainly not remain long enough even to attempt A levels. Now it may well be that the purposes of grammar school sixth forms include other things besides preparing pupils for A levels and University entrance. Be this as it may it is certainly one of the purposes of the sixth forms to do just these things, and the presence of even a small number of people who have no real interest in this objective can make it a difficult one to achieve. Yet it is rarely that such pupils are excluded. Few headmasters are so sure about what they are up to that they will refuse admission to the frankly unsuitable, and those who do try to do this may meet resistance from unexpected quarters.[1] It is therefore usual to admit them, arguing either that

[1] 'Members of Swansea Education Committee reported yesterday that about fourteen boys who failed to pass the General Certificate of Examination [sic] had been told to leave Bishop Gore grammar school, Swansea, by the headmaster.

'After a short discussion, in which several councillors said that parents had complained to them about the headmaster's action, the committee agreed that its chairman and deputy director of education should interview the headmaster – Dr. Ellis Lloyd – without delay and be given plenary powers to deal with the matter.

'The chairman of the committee, Mr. F. A. Gorst, said that no headmaster had any right to take such action. "We are responsible for the education of the children – not Dr. Lloyd or any other headmaster."

'Mr. J. Morgan Williams, a member of the Bishop Gore school staff, and a co-opted member of the education committee, said he knew how the boys were told to leave. He said that the fifth form were coming to the upper fifth. There were only nine or ten vacancies, and the headmaster had 28 boys who failed.

' "To deal with this problem you must create another form and get another

they may be 'late developers' or, seeing the matter from the point of view of those whose studies are going to be interfered with, that 'education is, after all, a matter of learning to live together'. And in case this should be thought over cynical then it must be admitted right away that trainers do exactly the same. The indulgence that the welfare professions extend to their clients encourages a similar indulgence towards students in training. There are accordingly strong pressures against getting rid of students, notwithstanding the strongest indications that many turn up from time to time, of unsuitable personality characteristics and even mental instability.

The double talk and intellectual confusion that is so marked a feature of present day educational comment is far removed from such an unequivocal statement as that of Thomas Arnold that 'the first duty of a schoolmaster is to get rid of unpromising subjects'. (Findlay, 1897. See Wymer, 1953, for a more recent account of Arnold's policy.) It would be difficult to exaggerate the importance in Arnold's system of the practice of 'superannuation'. It was not so much that Arnold weeded ruthlessly as that he removed plants of the wrong colour, cases for which the treatment was not suitable. No humiliation was involved in such a decision. 'To many he had removed he gave generous testimonials, and some he sent off with the advice that it was time they were at Oxford.' Arnold seems to have operated, a rare case among schoolmasters, as a virtuoso professional, judging situations in the light of expert knowledge, and acting with a complete autonomy. Doubtless such a policy could not have been pursued had he been subject to the many outside pressures, parental and governmental, with which the headmaster of a state school has to cope. But this is merely to emphasize the extent to which the attitude to information found among modern educationists is bound up with forms of government and control that would not

---

teacher. Dr. Lloyd was scrupulously fair in analysing the position. He did not want these boys out of school. There were about fourteen of them who did not have one subject. We have put some boys with four subjects in the sixth form this year. The solution, as far as I can make out, would be for a form with 28 boys."

'Mrs. Rose Cross, the deputy Mayor, said: "These boys should be back in school immediately." '

(*Manchester Guardian*, September 10th, 1958. I am indebted to Mr. F. B. Singleton, Librarian of the *Guardian*, for helping me to trace this news item.)

permit a headmaster to act on the basis of known probabilities even if he were to acknowledge them.

There is, finally, a sense in which legislation itself, and the fact finding processes that precede legislation (Royal Commissions, Advisory Committees) can be seen less as means of implementing specific ends than as forms of public testimony to ideas of what is good. Much legislation, and this perhaps applies especially to social service legislation, has an expressive as well as an instrumental aspect. And where the expressive aspect is dominant such legislation tends to be characterized by an absence of follow up measures, a reluctance to enquire whether legislation has been followed by changed practice, as though it were supposed that in the act of legislation itself reality is changed. Again, this has not always been the case. The formula of the Utilitarian philosophers was to examine, legislate and *inspect*. At both ends of the process appeal was made to facts. It was understood both that legislation had to acknowledge social realities, and that more than Divine Providence is needed if legislative provisions are to be translated into action. Even such a man as Shaftsbury understood that conditions in the asylums would not improve unless Commissioners paid surprise visits now and again. More than one commentator has noted the decline of fact collecting since that time, and one supposes that Professor O. R. McGregor's comments on 'the prevalent and pervasive confusion of the aims of welfare with the achievements of welfare' refer at least partly to a distinctive attitude to information, and to facts. Thus the welfare legislation of this century has often been, in no pejorative sense, Utopian. We have been concerned to build the good society, and legislators have been acutely conscious of being surrounded not by fellow technocrats but by friends and enemies. Certainly such legislation has often been polemical, and therefore doctrinaire, even when, as with the 1944 Education Act, the measure was agreed by all parties. The results of this act have already been discussed in Chapter II. Its provisions were not thought out operationally, i.e. in terms of what they would imply for finance and recruitment. To put the child-centred ideas of 1944 into practice would have required not only new schools, but also a type of teacher casework-oriented, working with small numbers and with total discretion. This did not happen. But a glance at the

stated purpose of the secondary modern schools as defined in the
Ministry pamphlet *The New Secondary Education*, 1948, suggests
that not even the ideas behind this particular provision reached
the level of articulate statement.[1] Taylor discusses this pamphlet
in some detail:

'The Ministry of Education pamphlet *The New Secondary Education*
made clear that the proper function of the Grammar school was to
provide a six- or seven-years' course, "regarded as a single whole
from eleven to eighteen, the earlier part of which should lead
naturally on to the later part and should no longer be conceived as a
course complete in itself to which a few pupils add an extra period of
one or two years". The same pamphlet suggested that Technical
schools differed "in fact from other types of secondary schools not
by being more closely related to 'life', but by selecting the sphere of
industry and commerce as their particular link with the adult world".
The vocational role of the Modern school, for reasons already suggested is hardly referred to except in the most imprecise and general
terms.'   (Taylor, 1963, pp. 18–19.)

It is quite clear that the concept of the secondary modern
school was from the first a residual category, to use the language of
formal logic. As a result the secondary modern schools are now
being dismantled for having become what many practitioners
said they would become, and paradoxically the task of setting up
a comprehensive system is being made all the more easy for the
fact that very few of the proposed *technical* schools ever got
started in the first place. The Crowther Report of 1959 has also
been mentioned (Chapter III). The recommendation that the
school-leaving age be raised to 16 was accompanied by no serious
examination of what exactly would be done with the 15-year-olds
who at the present time are glad to be gone, a circumstance
encouraged by the fact that no practising teacher was appointed
to that committee.

Nor of course is predominantly expressive legislation confined
to the field of education. The Criminal Justice Act of 1948 is now
under criticism partly because its provisions were in many cases
not thought through to the stage of implementation. The notion
of 'corrective training' in particular seems to have been the result
of mere verbal juxtaposition. The comment of one ex-corrective
trainee on this matter can scarcely be bettered:

[1] Above, chapter I, p. 3.

'Corrective training was an invention which was invented by a bodey of geezers, in the Home Office, when they brought out the new criminal justice act, whenever that was. When they had got it all nicely written down on paper, they handed it to the Home Secretary who presented it to the house. And they made a law, it was then handed to the prison commissioners who handed it down to the prison governors, who in their turn told the chief officers about it and they told the princeable officers, who ordered the screws to carry it out. This is all very nice except the only difference is they havn't got the first idea what it's all about.'

(Frank Norman, article in *Encounter*, May 1958.)
(The spelling is authentic.)

The tendency to regard Acts of Parliament as though they were the embodiment of ultimate truth contains within itself the seeds of disaster. For an Act is an artefact that embodies, sometimes only too clearly, not only the circumstances but also the political and philosophical assumptions of its day, and in a changing world these soon become out of date. But it is only rarely that provisions are made for periodic review, indeed the examination of basic premises may well be precluded for a considerable time after the act has been passed by the fact that these have become almost articles of faith. But to discourage realistic reappraisal is to encourage an unfortunate pattern of events. For in the absence of criticism events reach the point of complete breakdown before the seriousness of the situation is admitted. Inspection into the actual working of a policy, far from being a matter of course, tends then to take place in an atmosphere of astonishment and recrimination.

CHAPTER FIVE

Attitudes to Information in the Social Sciences: the Themes of Political Commitment and Reform

The theme has moved from that of the need for personal re-assurance into the wider area of political commitment and of reform movements. It is in these terms that it is most useful to examine the contributions to thinking on welfare provision made by social scientists themselves. The social sciences provide the theoretical rationale for the world of social policy. This means, however, that they too are inextricably intertwined with the spirit of high endeavour. The situation is changing as the social sciences become applied sciences in the service of industry and commerce, where performance criteria are more precise, but much academic sociology is exuberantly bound up with moral and political issues, a circumstance that materially affects the nature and quality of what social scientists *say*.

Ostensibly it is the function of academic comment to remove the component of value judgement in comment, to replace hunch by certainty. It is this intention that runs through the recent work of Mr. John Vaizey on the *economics* of education. The fact that every educational principle has a price tag on it is something we certainly needed to be reminded of. Yet in appraising academic comment we nonetheless encounter the problems that arise from the fact that academic people are after all human beings, with ethical and more particularly political convictions of their own. Most commonly we encounter the respect in which academic people, as representing the enlightened middle classes, tend to be 'liberal' and 'progressive' in outlook, and the respect in which the values of liberalism and reform sometimes contaminate their thinking. It is a commonplace that we are least rational about matters that touch us closest. For most of us this probably does not matter all that much. Custom draws a fairly sharp line between a man's public and his personal life, and although in his role as a chemist or an accountant he may be expected to be objective and detached no such requirements are made with regard to his personal affairs. (We would feel a bit uneasy if he did carry the same attitude into his private life.) But difficulties obviously arise when that man is a psychologist, or an economist or a sociologist. What happens when the professional concerns of the commentator impinge forcefully on his personal life and values? What happens, in particular, if that man has been attracted to the social sciences precisely because of his personal convictions about what is wrong with society and how its ills are to be cured? How is he to reconcile the roles of analyst and advocate?

The legal profession has met and apparently solved this matter of advocacy. A recent writer tells us:

'As far as matters of law are concerned the duty on the advocate is to bring to the attention of the court any and every relevant statute or decided case of which he has knowledge. It does not matter whether it is in his favour or not. In this instance his duty to the court dominates his duty to his client. . . . The rule is of great importance. Counsel are frequently called on to make "ex parte" applications, that is to present their case to a court when the other side are not present. . . . The courts then rely on counsel to draw their attention to the cases which are against the proposition they are advancing with as much care as those in favour of it.'

(Du Cann, 1964.)

Such a rule presumably ought to apply equally to the profession of scholarship. Charles Darwin is said to have noted in his margins every objection to the argument he was advancing that came to his mind. But it is probably easier to be objective about armadillos than about comprehensive schools. And there is another point, too, that although the difficulty that faces every social scientist of keeping his professional and his private identities apart has often been commented on, what has not so often been pointed out is that some social scientists might deny the propriety of even trying. When a social scientist contemplates his professional subject matter he may very well be doing so with loyalties evenly balanced, indeed his sense of certainty may be such that academic detachment appears very like dilettantism. The traditional teaching that convictions are one thing and science quite another has really no cogency in such a situation, indeed to assert this is only to invite attempts to dispense with the scientific ethic altogether.

And it is quite possible to do this. There are alternative solutions to the problem of the relationship between moral conviction and science. Typically these solutions are irrationalist in the sense that they claim to re-establish the place of conviction or of feelings, a place that it is felt has been wrongly usurped by mere reason. Such solutions are represented by the late-eighteenth-century philosophy of sensibility, by the popular radicalism of such people as Charles Dickens (his apostrophe to Tom Pinch expresses the spirit exactly), and by a tradition of historiography embodied in such writers as Carlyle and Belloc. Typically there is present a claim that so long as your heart is in the right place you cannot go far wrong. Exactly this feeling is strongly represented among social scientists, many of whom are, and some of whom even acknowledge themselves to be first and foremost activists. At a systematic level it is represented by the many varieties of thought, traceable ultimately to existentialism, that at the present time appear to claim a kind of legitimacy for convictions precisely on the grounds that they are strongly held. From this point of view to be *engagé*, far from being a disqualification, becomes almost the primary basis of valid comment.[1]

Another source of justification is to be found in sociology itself.[2] The sociology of knowledge can be used to cast doubt on the ultimate validity of the scientific ethic, and it will be pointed out that this ethic is a contingent phenomenon, an efflorescence of western civilization with close affinities to Puritanism; also that as the observer is necessarily the tenant of a unique status in a particular society his perceptions and therefore his notions of truth are inevitably both partial and unique. There is of course force in these arguments, though they seem to miss the point

[1] See Burns, 1960, Ch. IX, The revolt against intellect, pp. 291–299.

[2] The possibilities of sociology as a basis for irrationalist positions are recognized by Burns, op. cit. Durkheim is discussed under 'The revolt against intellect', Karl Mannheim as a founder of 'Twentieth Century Conservatism'. No reference is made however, to Mannheim's contributions to the sociology of knowledge, though this seems to me to be crucial.

that however much the outcome of history the scientific ethic has been substantially validated by performance; also that as an ethic it refers to aspirations, and that like any other aspiration it is not made nonsensical by the fact that we inevitably fall short of it. In any case it is certainly not a consequence of the sociology of knowledge that one assertion is as good as any other, or that the force with which a view is advanced, or the passion with which it is held contribute in some way to its validity.

But one would think this if one judged by the remarks that social scientists permit themselves when writing off the cuff, so to speak. So Mr. Vaizey, writing not about economics or about education but on the subject of institutional provision says this:

'It seems to me that one thing is in the nature of all institutions, whether they are for good purposes, like colleges, schools and hospitals, or for evil purposes, like prisons. Everyone in an institution is continually adapting himself to it, and to other people, whereas the glory of humanity is that it adapts its environment to mankind and not human beings to their environment. Civilization consists in deviation and difference. . . .'   (Vaizey, 1959, p. 104.)

It is difficult to believe that even someone not primarily identified as a sociologist can really mean this. The last people to maintain this position seriously were Rousseau and the Ideologues who followed him, and the least acquaintance with the history of thought since the French Revolution must suggest at least the possibility that the 'individual' is part product of his environment. All of which implies that as Mr. Vaizey is an eminent economist and educationist he probably does not mean it at all; he is merely airing his principles. This in turn provokes the reflection that the practice of parading one's political and moral position in the wrappings of factual statement is not all that uncommon.

The Ideologues too disliked institutions, and in the widest sense of the term:

'. . . the destruction of institutions was the high road towards . . . perfectibility, for to destroy institutions was to strike off the artificial fetters from the limbs of the natural man.'   (Elton, 1923.)

This is exactly what Mr. Vaizey is saying. The difference is that the Ideologues believed it while I do not think Mr. Vaizey really does. I think he is merely saying it. Now this is a pernicious

66

habit, and one into which liberal intellectuals too easily fall. It is bad because it deprives whole areas of human experience, on which progressive opinion has already made up its mind, of any sort of proper appraisal. Institutional provision is such an area, and one reason why realistic planning in this area is rather rare is no doubt that much published comment seems at the moment to be concerned more to establish the writer as a person of sensibility than to examine the problem. The habit betrays any writer who has fallen into it into progressively more absurd positions, for subsequent statements have to be made consistent with the initial premise. So, having decided that institutions are unequivocally bad Mr. Vaizey has to explain why we have them at all, and why people are willing to work in them. The strategy of his argument obliges him to stress not the perfectly obvious fact that institutional arrangements are a means of using scarce resources economically, nor the fact that institutional provision (as in schools and religous communities) has at times been thought to have positive merits, but to state:

'Above all . . . institutions give inadequate people what they want – power. Army officers, hospital sisters, prison warders – many of these people are inadequate and unfulfilled and they lust for power and control.'   (Op. cit. p. 108.)[1]

[1] In fairness to Mr. Vaizey it must be said that the first six chapters of his book, where he describes his personal experiences, seem to me to be essential reading for all who work in hospitals. It is with his analysis in Chapter VII, 'Why?' that I am inclined to quarrel, mainly because I think he encourages a sloppy way of thinking about institutional provision that has become very common, and I think it is the duty of academic people to set a good example in these matters. Compare, for example, the following passage from *Cambridge Opinion* for June 1964, a number devoted exclusively to '*Prisons*':

'There are some people whose presence in ordinary society arouses such anxiety or hostility or fear, or for whose welfare it is so unwilling to assume responsibility in its normal primary groups like the family, that special institutions were established to contain them: asylums for the insane, orphanages for homeless children, the workhouse for the poor and aged, barracks for the defenders of the state, prisons and reformatories for those who transgress and get caught. Discipline, routine, obedience and submission were the characteristics sought in the well-regulated institution, best obtained in an enclosed environment, away from the distractions, comforts, seductions and dangerous liberties of ordinary society. The nineteenth century was the great institution-building age – indeed the same characteristics were sought in the ordinary 'open' institutions of outside society, the factory, the school, the developing civil service, the patriarchal family. If for the 'progressives' of the early nineteenth century the aim was to tidy up society and get its aberrant or unfortunate members into institutions, the

There is obviously a lot of truth in this. People do sometimes go in for institutional work for just these reasons, and we have all known them. But the lust for power and control is an attribute of human beings as such and one – Mr. Vaizey must surely see this – that is equally capable of being satisfied by becoming a reformer or a don.

Specialist comment avoids the more obvious forms of self-indulgence as a rule, yet is often marked by a distaste for the subject matter that subtly influences the sorts of thing that are said, the way they are said, and the general cast of theory. Even the Morrises' excellent study of Pentonville Prison (T. and P. Morris, 1963) can be faulted on these grounds, I think. Like Mr. Vaizey the authors rely heavily on human folly and inadequacy as an explanatory principle, the folly of society in permitting the kinds of condition they found, and the inadequacy of people within the organization in not doing better than they did. Thus I think it is partly the strategy of their argument that leads them to stress on more than one occasion the common cultural heritage of Pentonville uniformed staff and Pentonville prisoners, and to entertain the possibility that Pentonville officers were inferior to those found elsewhere in the prison service (pp. 98–101). These things may have been true; the fact is that these are not strong arguments to use in any explanation of the deplorable conditions they found. The changed attitudes that have followed organizational change elsewhere in the prison service (and in the hospital service) suggest that bad staff are nowhere as much of a problem as bad systems. It is not that the Morrises underestimate organizational problems. This is what much of the book is about. It is rather that the authors are telling us about the absurd and astonishing things that go on while leaving me, at least, still uncertain about why they go on other than that someone or other allows them to, and I do not think this is an explanation.

---

progressive task of our own day is to get them out again. In the last fifteen or twenty years a literature has grown up which both reflects and nourishes a new theory of institutions: that they are no good.'

There are several indications here – the repeated and imprecise use of words like 'ordinary', 'normal' and 'open', the tired joke in line six – that the writer has simply been misled about the standard required of serious social commentary. The argument is very similar to Mr. Vaizey's. The explanation is again quasi-clinical in nature, though the locus of pathology is now said to be in 'society' rather than in practitioners. There is no hint of any real acquaintance with the many different factors encouraging institutional provision over the past two hundred years.

Perhaps more than any other social science criminology tends to be approached from a standpoint that is essentially *reformist*. In their private capacities criminologists seem to be penal reformers almost to a man (but see this chapter, p.72). There is nothing wrong in this; a criminologist is as entitled to have a private capacity as the next man. But it is difficult to confine a reformist disposition to one's private capacity, and one suspects that criminology may sometimes attract those who are reformers first and scientists second. Dr. Howard Jones has gone so far as to assure us that criminology is 'above all . . . a reformist study' (Jones, 1962, p. 1). But this suggests that criminology is a pursuit in which personal convictions and professional concern come so close as to involve any criminologist who maintains this position in problems of acute role conflict. For it is difficult to see how any social scientist can operate as an observer and diagnostician of the very society of which he is an explicitly committed member without the quality of his analyses being seriously affected.

The role of the social scientist in applied fields

In fact the problems raised by the ambiguity of the social scientist's position resolve themselves into a choice. In what capacity is he to operate if he is going to work in an applied field? There are two possibilities. He can either accept as given the social setting within which he is working, and the values of the society of which it is part, and concern himself with topics of strictly limited scope like any other hired hand. Or else he can take nothing for granted and regard society, his work setting and even his colleagues as proper objects of study. In practice the problem arises in multi-disciplinary research in connection with the social scientist's attitude to the research task and to his colleagues from other disciplines. Thus, granted that it is because of particular *social* problems that he is present at all there still remains the question of whether he is to regard these problems, and the terms in which they are stated, as his own problems and his own terms of reference. Or is he, on the other hand, to regard not merely the problems but the terms in which they are stated, and the fact that one range of problems was thought worth looking at and not another, as facts themselves needing to be thought about. Similarly what view is he to adopt of his col-

F   69

laborators, the practitioners (psychiatrists, industrialists, prison officials), whose practical concerns brought the research into being, and of his own role in relation to them? Insofar as he is only there at all because of their need for him there are obvious reasons for his regarding them, at least at the outset, as equal partners in a joint enterprise. At the same time, however, there are obvious considerations to do with the very subject matter of sociology why it might be more proper to regard them from quite another point of view, as objects of study in themselves.

In the first position the sociologist is cast in the role of consultant expert, limiting his attention strictly to the immediate problem, and taking no account of wider theoretical issues. In this kind of role the sociologist may act as technical adviser, as for example, in the design of research instruments. This may be called the role of staff sociologist. In the second position, however, the social scientist claims as his focus a much wider range of human activity, including perhaps the practice of setting up interdisciplinary research teams and the possible roles of their members. In the medical field, for example, such a standpoint would enable him to study not only the social environments of people defined by others as 'sick' but also the circumstances in which the label of 'sickness' gets attached to some forms of deviant behaviour and not to others. Similarly in the criminological field such a standpoint would enable him to study not only the criminal but also the social setting in which the criminal emerges, is labelled as criminal, handled and is studied. This may be called the role of academic sociologist.[1]

Ultimately these roles are almost certainly not incompatible, but at the present stage in the evolution of research organization it generally appears that a choice has to be made, and there are in fact cogent arguments for each position. Foremost among the arguments in favour of a staff role is the matter of expertise. In medical/social science collaboration statements by medical men

[1] C.f. A. W. Gouldner's distinction between 'engineering' and 'clinical' approaches (Gouldner, 1956). The former is characterised by the fact that the client's formulation of the problem is accepted by the sociologist, who is concerned only to discover efficient ways of solving the problem; the latter by the fact that the sociologist . . . is not restricted, and is generally recognised as not being restricted, to the client's own definition of the problem, which he may indeed regard as one of the symptoms of the underlying difficulties. (Bottomore, 1962).

on medical matters seem inevitably exempt from very much in the way of outside comment. Hence in epidemiological research work is commonly organized at least at the outset into different departments, clinical and sociological, each with its proper subject·matter between which *correlations* are typically sought. Such research works quite well without either side impinging on the other. The analogous situation in criminology would be one where the social scientist, accepting the definition of certain acts as 'criminal' investigated such matters as the prevalence of such acts in particular groups. Epidemiology could presumably be organized in much the same way as in medical research. Or else accepting the goal of some particular form of provision to be, say, rehabilitation, he might examine the extent to which this goal was achieved, or study which forms of organization were most likely to achieve it. In either case the criminologist would occupy a kind of staff position in the world of penal policy. Such a position seems to be implicit in the suggestion that the problems of penal policy be investigated by the methods of operational research (Wilkins, 1962). It is an entirely familiar position, for it is part of the traditional role of the scientist that he is concerned with means and not with ends. 'Tell me what you want to do,' he says, 'and I will suggest how you might be able to do it.'

But although this position is at the moment being recommended to criminologists the fact that the status of operational research worker seems so novel indicates that it is not the way criminologists habitually think of themselves. In fact criminologists as a rule do not work this way at all. Far from accepting as given the contexts within which they operate they tend to be deeply concerned with the context itself. Far from accepting as given the assurance that certain acts are crimes and pursuing their research from that point on criminologists seem to be very much in the habit of asking why certain acts are labelled crimes and others not, and from time to time questioning the sense of the labelling system. Nor are they disposed to take for granted organizational goals in quite the way that an operational research worker would be required to do. While a criminologist might well work happily on the problem of how to implement a remedial policy it is difficult to image many criminologists working with similar enthusiasm on how to make the experience of a detention centre short, sharp and shocking.

The relationships between social scientist and practitioner, social science and *society*, seems then to be different from that found in medical/social science collaboration. The field of law enforcement is obviously one that raises moral issues obtrusively, though it would be a mistake to suppose that similar issues are absent in the medical field, or even that the two fields are in any ultimate sense different. It may be that in law enforcement they are merely nearer the surface. There are in fact other reasons for the peculiar relationships between social scientist and practitioner in the field of law enforcement and, for that matter, such fields as education. The possession of esoteric knowledge by medical colleagues encourages the sociologist to accept perhaps quite gratefully, the role of expert in the social aspects of a 'medicine' that is not itself subject to scrutiny. He is still, to put the matter bluntly, the junior partner. But in criminology (and education) there is lacking any form of demonstrable expertise or esoteric knowledge on the part of the practitioner. The social scientist, feeling himself to be the only expert present, is accordingly tempted to make more extensive claims, and thinks it entirely proper to extend to the practitioner the same kind of scrutiny that he gives to the client.

It might be argued that for a social scientist not to adopt such a detached view of the scene would be to limit his subject matter in a way that has nothing to warrant it if sociology is the study of social phenomena and not merely of some. For prison officials are as much part of society as prisoners. Is this why the criminologist claims a role more comprehensive than that of staff adviser? It would certainly be to locate criminology in the main sociological tradition if it were defined as the sociology of law enforcement, and in fact one criminologist does exactly this. Dr. Nigel Walker defines his recent book on *Crime and Punishment in Britain* (1965) as 'a study of our present ways of defining, accounting for, and disposing of offenders, regarded simply as a system in operation. To the extent that the book succeeds in adhering to this ascetic principle it is a work of criminology'. Dr. Walker is in fact concerned to establish that criminology, as he sees it, is not a matter of moral or political philosophy, nor is the criminologist properly a penal reformer. I have no doubt that there are other criminologists who share Dr. Walker's views, and to the extent that this is true then I must apologize for lumping all criminologists together in the discussion so far. But this asceticism is born of a self consciousness that is, I think, rather new, and certainly there are many criminologists in England who would wholeheartedly endorse Dr. Howard Jones' alternative definition. It is with this school in mind that the present argument proceeds.

Dr. Walker's definition of criminology would give scope to study not only the aetiology of 'crimes' but also the circumstances in which one kind of act gets defined as a crime and another not. It would become equally the business of criminology to study both the efficacy of particular forms of penal treatment and also the social circumstances in which a goal of treatment emerges in preference to other goals. Not least important it would become possible to study the total influences brought to bear in the framing of penal policy, the composition and beliefs of all pressure groups including not only the police, the judiciary and the general public but also the liberal press, the reform organizations and the universities.

But criminologists do not do this. The aetiology of criminal behaviour is a primary preoccupation, the focus of much theoretical activity of a psychoanalytic kind at the moment; the social machinery is interesting only to the extent that it permits gleeful remarks that the criminal is, after all, only the one who gets caught, or that middle class delinquents do not get prosecuted. Similarly the efficacy of particular forms of treatment is a regular subject for discussion, the choice of a goal of treatment is taken entirely for granted. The beliefs and values of the police, the judiciary and the general public are under constant scrutiny; the beliefs and values of penal reformers and lecturers in criminology go entirely unconsidered. Now there is significance in the kind of questions we ask, and the things we let go unexplored, and it is clear that the topics that are not in fact explored have at least one thing in common: they all suppose a readiness to enquire into aspects of contemporary society to a point where doubt might begin to be cast on aspects of contemporary values that many criminologists and other social scientists would suppose to be the premises from which enquiry begins. Discussions of criminology do as a rule devote some space to the fact that categories of crime vary from society to society, but this is typically handled within the framework of an implicit evolutionism, rarely by relating variations to social and political circumstances Similarly the policy of 'treatment', if discussed at all, is generally assumed to be 'scientific' in nature, or otherwise the culmination of social progress; rarely is there a hint that the choice of one policy rather than another might be explained in terms of the political, economic and social circumstances of the society making the choice. Least of all does one find any attempt by criminologists to appraise their own circumstances, their own sources of recruitment and characteristic ethical and political orientations. Yet this would not be an absurd thing to ask. It is, after all, a mark of any competent social scientist that he should be able to diagnose his own situation.

It would, of course, be foolish to underestimate the difficulty of keeping apart the roles of actor and observer in such a contentious area as that of law enforcement. None the less the result of not doing so is confusion. For of the two positions which, as a social scientist, the criminologist might usefully adopt he seems often unable to choose either. The position of staff sociologist may involve the acceptance of ideas and values that in his private capacity he finds distasteful; the position of academic sociologist the questioning of ideas and values that in his private capacity he feels to be self-evident. The result is often a hopping-about from one capacity to another and back again which renders criminological arguments so often difficult to evaluate or even to follow. Discussions of the meaning or use of the word 'crime' provide a perfect example of this kind of thing.

'What is crime?'

The problem of how this word is to be used is one that is readily solvable by the adoption of a sufficiently detached standpoint but one that remains unsolved because the adoption of such a standpoint would be destructive of prevailing ethical assumptions. To put the matter another way solutions readily available to the criminologist in his capacity as a social scientist are unacceptable to him in his capacity as a citizen. They are on that account discounted, and the resulting impasse attributed to the supposedly intractable nature of sociological material, when in fact it is due to the standpoint from which the material is being viewed.

The problem of what crime 'is' crops up in various ways.

The relativity of legal definitions offers material for speculation. Thus Dr. Howard Jones remarks:

'. . . what is forbidden by the law changes from year to year, and is impressively transformed over longer periods, or at times of social upheaval such as war or revolution. In the eighteenth century, the death penalty was imposed for all sorts of trivial acts: appearing disguised on the public highway, shooting rabbits, "stealing anything privily from a person". And while murder was treated with great tolerance, it was a capital offence to slit a person's nose. . . .

Similar striking differences in the penal code occur between different countries, even countries with the same general heritage of culture. Thus homosexuality between men, which is such a serious offence in England, is ignored in France and parts of Scandinavia. Differences multiply as one crosses cultural boundaries: bigamy is an offence in the west, but in some Arab countries and in many primitive communities, polygamy is an established social institution.'

(Jones, op. cit., pp. 3–4.)

The problem becomes of practical importance in research, particularly quantitative research, where it may be necessary to establish the absolute incidence of crime for the purpose of comparing crime rates. It then becomes crucially necessary to know what to count as a case. And this is where the debate begins, because what to one observer is 'obviously a crime' may be to another 'not really a crime at all'. (The identical problem arises in psychiatric epidemiology.) Thus Dr. Jones postulates a category of persistent offenders who are 'perhaps not really criminals' and elsewhere suggests that 'much of the anti-social behaviour which finds its way into the criminal statistics is not really crime at all'. In the framing of such remarks Dr. Jones is clearly postulating a sort of entity, 'crime', that transcends historical and regional differences and the vicissitudes of criminal statistics. The conviction that notwithstanding such variations there is a *thing* which we call Crime, elusive but nonetheless existent, takes its place along with similar convictions about the existence of other things called Education, Health and the like. (This way of thinking is crucially connected with the habit of defining objectives in global terms, for it is on the presumed existence of Education, Health and so on that the practice rests.) Such convictions form the basis of classical essentialist philosophies traceable ultimately to Plato. The essentialist solution to these problems appears to involve an act of contemplation with a view to determining what are the 'essential' attributes of the entity in question. Its processes are frankly obscure, yet can generally be detected by the use of such words as 'essential', 'natural' or 'really', as when it is suggested that homosexuality is not really a crime, or that juvenile delinquents are not really criminals. Essentialist positions have been severely, and one would suppose fatally undermined by contempory schools of linguistic philosophy; comparative material from the social anthropologist and historian has similarly exposed the ethnocentrism that lies at the heart of such arguments. Dr. Jones' criticism of the ninteenth-century criminologist Garofalo is in fact a criticism of the essentialist method. Garofalo solved the problem of what crime 'really is' by speaking of 'natural crime':

> 'Natural crimes . . . are acts which do violence to certain essential characteristics of human nature and human social life. They include behaviour which runs counter to the natural human sentiments of compassion or honesty, or which are harmful to the community.'
>
> (Ibid, p. 4.)

Unfortunately, as Dr. Jones points out, the objectivity of such concepts is only apparent. Ideas like this betray an ignorance of the variability of human nature institutions as revealed by both historical and anthropological research, and it is not necessary to examine them for very long before discovering that they rest on the writer's own notions of morality.

Faced with the fact of cultural variability many writers have concluded that to postulate entities that are not found empirically in any known society is a mere verbal exercise, designed only to support one's own ethical convictions. In practice, in any given society, the only material we have to go on is information about what the criminal law in fact forbids. From this consideration emerges the solution of radical relativism, a position character-ised by a refusal to attempt any form of absolute definition whatever. Thus G. B. Vold seems to argue that crime is whatever is against the criminal law in whatever the society under dis-cussion.[1] As Dr. Jones puts it, 'Acts not socially defined as criminal

---

[1] It is not entirely clear what Vold's position is on this point. In his discussion of 'White Collar Crime' he seems to argue against strictly legal definitions. Thus: 'The label results in good part from the semantic device of calling all violations of law or regulations "crime" and all persons involved "criminals" (Vold, p. 254.) Never-

are not in fact criminal, for it is legal proscription which makes crime a crime,' (Op. cit., p. 101.) Such radically empirical solutions are familiar to anthropologists and philosophers alike. The problem is solved by looking at it not from the standpoint of a member of society but as if from outside. This, of course, is a method that in the study of non-European societies is not only admitted to be illuminating but also felt to be entirely proper. Used in the analysis of one's own society however, it suggests an attitude of non-involvement that borders on downright rejection. It is not therefore likely to appeal to anyone deeply concerned to establish a definition of crime that will serve as a guide to social policy. The problem is solved, but it is solved by demonstration that it is in fact a pseudo problem, a verbal puzzle. This is not flattering to those who have seen it as real, and urgent. Strictly philosophical solutions do not find favour with social scientists who are actively engaged in building a better world, for they put a stop to speculation in a manner that brings us sharply up against the fact that in the furthering of this policy or that, even in the pursuit of such apparently ultimate things as medical treatment, we act not as agents of some ultimate truth but as creatures of our own time and place. And this, clearly is a profoundly undermining reflection for many people. Hence the curious double standard by which many social scientists seem to operate. The objectivity which is regarded as essential in the study of non-European societies is somehow felt to be frivolous and reprehensible when extended to one's own. So Dr. Jones rejects Vold's solution without refuting it, for his use of a kind of statistical argument in rebuttal is not sound. His position on this particular issue indeed

---

theless in the course of his discussion of 'social conflict' theories of criminality Jones quotes Vold as saying: 'In other words, the whole political process of law-making, law-breaking and law-enforcement becomes a direct reflection of deep seated and fundamental conflict between interest groups and their more general struggles for the control of the police power of the State. Those who produce legislative majorities win control over the police power and dominate the policies that decide who is likely to be involved in violation of the law.' (Ibid, pp. 208–209.) It seems clear that in such a Marxian analysis of the genesis of crime is implied a statement about the status of the term 'Crime', and one that is entirely consistent with the 'semantic device' of reserving it to denote violations of the law. I am therefore inclined to think that Jones is correct in seeing this particular passage as involving support of a strictly legal definition of crime. I am obliged to Professor Sprott for pointing out this difficulty.

77

typifies the equivocal position in which many social scientists find themselves: Vold's solution, the most plausible, he seems to find ethically unsatisfying; Garofalo's concept of natural crime, the most ethically satisfying, the one that comes nearest to providing a form of *personal* guidance, he finds implausible. Yet his own position is nearer to that of Garofalo than to Vold. Having shown that the idea of natural crime is unsound he nevertheless proceeds on the assumption that absolute definitions are possible. The question 'what is crime' remains unanswered but, it is implied, is capable of being answered. This is a typically essentialist position, to suppose that questions like 'what is crime', 'what is education', 'what is health', 'what is a psychopath'[1] are difficult but meaningful, and difficult because of the supposed complexity of the material. Yet a rigorously sociological approach, or a semantic approach, or a philosophical approach in the pragmatic tradition would suggest that such questions are unanswerable because meaningless, except in the purely limited sense of what forms the definition of crime takes in whatever is the society under discussion. It is only because the criminologist confuses his role as a citizen with his role as a scientist that such questions appear so perplexing. From a strictly sociological standpoint they present no difficulties at all. Yet this is only to draw attention to the immense difficulties of maintaining a strictly sociological standpoint, and to the fact that as committed members of society our attitudes to information must be to some extent equivocal, no matter who we are.

Discussions of the nature of crime reveal the difficulties that face the social scientist by virtue of the fact that he is also a committed member of a society, and on that account concerned with problems in a way that is simultaneously analytical and moral. Discussions of actual penal policy reveal the more obdurate problems that arise when the social scientist is explicity committed as a reformer. This is nowhere so marked as in discussions of the principles of retribution on the one hand and 'treatment' on the other.

Discussions of retribution and treatment

These are matters on which criminologists are likely to have settled opinions. Sometimes the element of commitment is

[1] Or 'what is a profession?' See Chapter II, p. 17, Note 1, above.

acknowledged. Dr. Jones, for example, maintains that criminology is 'above all a reformist study' (above, p. 69). Yet he also
assures us that scientists must pursue their activities 'free from
any preconceived ethical notions' (op. cit., p. 3). This is a profoundly ambiguous position that reveals itself in what Dr. Jones
has to say about retribution:

> 'The retributive motive . . . focuses attention upon the offence rather
> than the offender, and so is doggedly opposed to any scientific
> approach, aimed at the individual delinquent and intended to deter
> him from further delinquencies or to reform him.' (Ibid, p. 138.)

Here the commitment to the principles of deterrence and
reform would seem to be entirely matters of personal choice,
yet a claim is clearly being made that the principles of deterrence
and reform are in some sense 'scientific' while that of retribution
is not. And it is obvious that this claim must be made in order to
reconcile the proposition that criminology is a reformist science
with the proposition that scientific activity is ethically neutral.
Clearly reform must be shown to be itself *scientific*. What weight
is such an assertion?

It is certainly possible to bring together the realms of fact and
obligation, as we have seen (above, p. 65). Existentialism provides
one solution by assuring us that what we feel strongly must be
in some sense also 'true'. Far older is the tradition of Natural Law,
again traceable to Plato, by which considerations of fact are felt
to furnish guidance about what is desirable. Many social scientists do in fact appear to be believers in Natural Law insofar as
they appear to believe that what is ethically desirable can only be
desirable to the extent that it is rooted in empirical investigation;
more familiarly that investigation can itself give us guidance
about what we ought to do. At its best the position is based on a
belief that reason and ethics alike stem from the same divine or
natural order, and that there cannot accordingly be any conflict
between them. The position is potentially dangerous, however,
for while traditionally the task has been seen as that of attempting
to reach ethical certainties by a process of reasoning from known
facts, it is clearly possible to proceed in the opposite direction and
deduce from supposedly unassailable first premises conclusions
about what must factually be the case. Here natural law and ex-
istentialist positions meet.

It seems to be this kind of thinking that underlies the kind of argument discussed in the last chapter. In penal policy it is this that no doubt underlies the disposition of many commentators to proceed from such a premise as that psychotherapy (or probation, or group counselling, or social case-work) is a good and humane way of dealing with offenders to the conclusion that it is also effective, or that it would be if it were tried. A confusion between desirability and effectiveness is indeed almost distinctive of the correctional field so that it is generally believed not only that what is agreed to be desirable in penal policy can only be desirable insofar as it can be shown to be effective in some particular direction, but also that what is agreed to be desirable must inevitably be effective because it is desirable. Few voices, only those of the operational research workers are raised to question these articles of faith (above, Chapter III, p. 40). The danger in a belief that reason and ethics cannot but be consistent is clearly that in the presence of strong convictions it effectively dispenses with the need for enquiry altogether. This is no doubt why some questions are simply not asked.

However a belief that policies can be dictated by facts alone, by 'science' has now to be given some kind of extended justification, for not since the days of David Hume has it been possible to take it for granted. And if at the present time there are many social scientists who believe that ethics must be based on science there are also a good many people who believe that to suppose this, or to suppose that science obliges us to do any one thing rather than another is to betray a misunderstanding not only of what science is about, but also of what constitutes a moral judgement.

It is at least arguable that if we choose to take account of the welfare of the individual in penal policy rather than the welfare of society then this is a matter on which science has nothing at all to say. Hume advanced reasons for thinking that no amount of contemplating what is the case can ever tell us what ought to be the case, or how we ought to act. The least philosophical of us cannot but be aware that the argument at least exists. Many people think that Hume was right. It may be, however, that he was wrong, and that those who think like him are wrong. It is certain, however, that anyone who believes that a science of criminology has 'reformist' aims, or that the cause of reform is in any way sanctified by science must show that he was wrong. It is too late in the day for the argument to be ignored.

The fact is, however, that many social scientists seem to equate the worlds of science and ethics insofar as when they are not saying that the moral framework can be dispensed with altogether they are implying that the arguments for or against particular policies can only be advanced on instrumental grounds, in terms of their measurable effectiveness towards particular ends. But this is to encounter the difficulty that only a moral argument can be advanced for some of the policies that enlightened opinion would approve, for not every policy aimed at the reform of the offender is measurably effective. In the absence of any known measures of efficacy the most that can be said for such policies as group counselling and psychotherapy is that they represent ways of dealing with people that we feel to be right and proper. This is enough to justify the policy. But a purely instrumental approach is unable to use such arguments, so inevitably such policies get credited with a pragmatic effectiveness that it is by no means certain they have.

This avoidance of moral, even of expressive, arguments has been only too apparent in the way criminologists have handled the matter of capital punishment; indeed it has materially affected the quality of their contribution to the debate. For if Hume is right then the question of deterrence on which the argument has invariably focused is entirely irrelevant to the main issue. It has surely been the determination of the reformers to secure the abolition of capital punishment quite as much as that of their opponents to retain it that has made it tactically impossible to recognize the irrelevance of merely prudential arguments to either side. Thus if I feel capital punishment to be wrong it is simply not to the point to argue that it is an effective deterrent, nor is it to the point that it is ineffective if I happen to feel that murder is so loathsome a crime as to merit signal disapproval. Moral judgements simply are not to be established, nor are they to be answered in this way. To suppose otherwise is to confuse morality with expediency, and such confusion is found in the most unexpected quarters. Thus the Catholic authors of a recent argument for the abolition of the death penalty state that 'the death penalty for murder in this country at present is unnecessary and therefore unjust' (Tidmarsh et al., 1963). But it is, of course, perfectly possible to argue that it would be unjust were it even 'necessary' – presumably as an effective deterrent – or that it is just and right even though ineffective. The question of deterrence is from this standpoint a matter of contingencies that does not really enter into the argument. The practical consequence of whatever policy ultimately prevails is simply the price we have to pay for the right to have moral principles at all, and the price of moral principles may be extreme personal inconvenience to the ultimate point of martyrdom.

The implications, then, of what is an entirely plausible theoretical position are that there never was a compelling or 'scientific' argument for the abolition of capital punishment, nor one for retention, nor one for any other penal policy, or any other policy either. On the matter of capital punishment there are cogent moral arguments either way, and in the last analysis the decision to abolish or retain is misrepresented if it appears in the guise of a triumph of reason or of a defeat. It is simply a matter of who is to be master. This may be untidy, but it is the way society in fact works. The issue of capital punishment is perhaps the one that has most confused the study of criminology and prevented the emergence of that candour that is one of the marks of mature discipline. Precisely because this is a matter on which they feel most strongly this issue, and the issue of punishment generally, is one on which few criminologists seem able even to maintain a coherent train of thought. One of the by-products of the abolition of capital punishment may well be an improvement in the quality of criminological discussion in this area.

And yet perhaps not, for there is an inherent paradox in the very position of social scientists who wish to harness their expertise to instrumental ends. For the instrumental approach involves the denial of whole areas of social science thought, in particular thought on the matter of the element of *order* in society. Social scientists appear to have a somewhat equivocal attitude to the insights and subject matter of sociology itself.

The use of sociology by social scientist reformers

Thus suppose it were possible to invoke the name of science to lend a kind of support to ethical preferences one might ask how matters then stood. Do scientific considerations lend support more to the cause of rehabilitation or more to that of retribution? Everything depends on which sciences one has in mind. The fact is, however, that the specifically social sciences, sociology itself most conspicuously, seem to lend themselves more easily to the retributionists than to the reformer. The principle of retribution takes no account of the individual's welfare admittedly, but it does consider the interests of society. So Dr. Jones marshals a formidable array of witnesses to the fact that the retributive element in court disposals functions as an affirmation of society's values. He quotes the dictum of Professor Goodheart that:

> 'retribution in punishment is an expression of the community's disapproval of crime, and if this retribution is not given recognition then the disapproval may also disappear.' (Jones, op. cit., p. 136.)

This argument is recognizably sociological in nature, and therefore one that a sociologist might be expected to be familiar with and to treat with some respect. It is in fact a theory of punishment specifically associated in sociology with the name of Durkheim, who went so far as to argue that crime is an essential aspect of social life as it is in the act of punishment that society's values are reaffirmed. But this is to create difficulty for any social scientist who has seen his proper contribution to be in providing insights into how specific instrumental objectives are to be achieved, particularly if he has identified himself with a limited number of such possible objectives, i.e. reform, and most particularly if in his mind reform is equated with the pursuit of individualized treatment.

The difficulty of his situation is exemplified by Dr. Jones' handling of this particular point, for he has no more to say of Professor Goodheart's argument than that it is 'dubious' (Ibid. p. 136.) Nor does he mean that the argument is morally dubious, as he is perfectly entitled to claim if he wishes, but that Goodheart's argument, and Durkheim's are unsound as arguments. But he does not say where the unsoundness lies. Instead he adopts an oddly high handed tone with those jurists who in maintaining the symbolic or communicative function of punishment reveal an intimate understanding of what is involved in sociological thinking. The argument seems on the face of it to be worthy of consideration, yet it is not answered, nor even seriously discussed. Instead Dr. Jones advances two objections to Goodheart's position, that in view of the subjective nature of suffering the amount of pain suffered cannot be graduated in relation to the heinousness of the offence; secondly that it cannot be good to inflict pain. The first objection sadly illustrates the tactics of criminological discussion in contentious areas for it is simply irrelevant to the point being made. The question of how much pain is suffered has no bearing on the argument for the symbolic value of punishment. Insofar as the element of retribution functions as a statement of public morality it is centrally concerned with the definition of prohibited *acts*, and that these be met with *acts* of punishment. In neither case does the question of states of mind arise. Dr. Jones may feel that this is improper, and has a perfect right to say so, but this is not equivalent to demolishing the argument. To his second objection it is equally possible to reply that in actual social life we have to content ourselves with only proximate goals, if only because interests are so often opposed. Dr. Jones' position is that of the consultant who, in refusing to recognize that he operates within a financial and administrative framework insists that the interests of his patient must come first, and so monopolizes resources that he severely handicaps the hospital. Including, of course, all the other patients, and this is the point where the individualist position is at its weakest. Goodheart is prepared to see the individual suffer for the good of society; Jones is prepared to see society suffer for the good of the individual. But 'society' is only a shorthand word. 'Society' is composed of individuals, and it is in principle possible to imagine each individual as the protégé of Dr. Jones, or myself, or some other social scientist. What then? It is clear that when Jones talks about the individual he means the individual I happen to have met, or be acquainted with or be interested in. But this is not a sufficient basis for a viable social philosophy.

The grounds for an assertion that retribution is dubious can in fact only be moral ones. There are no sociological grounds for holding this position, indeed sociological arguments, insofar as they can be said to support any proposals for action, tend rather to the contrary. At various points in his book, however, there are indications that the scientific grounds to which Dr. Jones alludes are in fact not sociological but psychoanalytic. Concern with retribution, he argues, is irrationally motivated, and discreditably at that:

'We all seem to need a scapegoat on to whom we can project our own hatred and feelings of guilt.'

(Ibid., p. 9.)

'The chief obstacle to further progress is going to be not the moral question, for as the psychoanalysts have shown this is very largely a rationalisation, but our own need for a scapegoat on to whom we can erupt the hostile feelings pent within us all.'

(Ibid., p. 138.)

But it is, of course, debatable whether the psychoanalysts have *shown* anything of the sort. It is true that psychoanalysts have from time to time asserted that moral judgements are largely rationalizations for unconscious and often discreditable motives, and this may often be the case. But it is equally possible that they represent society's quite sensible and rational attempts to preserve itself, which is a possibility one might expect a sociologist at least to acknowledge. In any case the assertion that moral judgements are irrationally motivated involves anyone who makes it in a logically untenable position, for notwithstanding his rejection of a moral standpoint the criminologist, when making recommendations, is necessarily adopting one. For example a sentiment frequently expressed by some criminologists is that in court disposals 'we might do better to try to steer the punishment or treatment of offenders right away from moral issues' (Dr. Terence Morris, reviewing a book by Lord Longford). But it is difficult to believe that a sociologist can mean a statement like this to be taken seriously. If he does then one can only wonder whether sociologists working in the field of penal policy really appreciate what sociology is about. In any case it is fairly obvious that to recommend that court disposals be decided solely in the light of the offender's needs is to adopt a moral position on the matter of court disposals. It may even be a *more* moral position, but it is a moral position for all that. Similarly Dr. Jones is entitled to believe that concern with retribution is wrong, and that reform and therapy are the only decent and proper objectives in penal policy, but such beliefs are held in his private capacity only. The fact that he holds these beliefs very strongly, and even the fact that probably most other criminologists think like him gives him no warrant for claiming that they have the backing of science, or that deterrence is 'the real aim of the criminologist' (Ibid., p. 139).

Attitudes to Information in the Social Sciences

The flight from social relationships

In the field of social welfare, then, the theorist seems to be no more able than the practitioner to maintain the entirely dispassionate attitude towards information that marks the virtuoso professional. This ought not to be surprising. The field of social policy is one that inevitably concerns us as moral beings, and it would not be necessary to go into this amount of detail were it not for the daily appearance of claims that the incursion of social science expertise into an area of human life renders its processes morally neutral. The social scientist sets out to improve on the practitioner's perceptions of reality. He agrees with everything we have to say about bias and self deception among practitioners, and proposes to replace this by accurate knowledge. But at the end of the day what we seem to find is no sort of limpid objectivity, but rather the exploitation of selected areas of social science thought in pursuit of unacknowledged political programmes.[1] Certainly the impropriety of doing this is acknowledged by social scientists, but with the result not that they acknowledge the programmes, but that they attempt to regularize their position by claiming that the programmes (the assault on institutional provision, the individualization of penal treatment) are themselves dictated by science. But this is an illusion, and one is left wondering why it should be so manifestly impossible for so many scientists to acknowledge the legitimacy of moral objectives in the pursuit of which science could quite properly be harnessed. Why, in short, cannot the unacknowledged be acknowledged?

Certainly the failure of even social scientists to conduct the

---

[1] This seems to be the invariable fate of social scientists who have based their working principles on the somewhat naïve epistemology of the Positivist tradition. Auguste Comte, founder of Positivism, survives to be classed by E. M. Burns as an 'anti-intellectual' (Burns, 1960, p. 305); Durkheim, who warned his followers to beware of their own preconceptions and prejudices, to be discussed as part of 'the revolt against intellect' (ibid., p. 280). Burns is not entirely fair to these early sociologists in that he often reads statements of observed fact as prescriptive. Durkheim's insight into the social nature of thought ('representations') is in no sense equivalent to an 'adulation of society' (ibid., p. 281). Nevertheless Positivist sociology, like all deterministic theories, has yet to explain why its own formulations are exempt from otherwise general rules of its own making. It was Pareto, also a Positivist, who stressed the element of rationalization in systematic thinking, yet it is easy to see how the idea of a purely instrumental social science has political value for social scientists, as I hope to show (Chapter VII).

discussion of social policy in terms that are in any recognizable sense scientific seems to testify to something irreducibly non-rational about social policy. Such a conclusion accords with the similar inability of practitioners to acknowledge facts, as with their aversion to setting strictly limited objectives and making use of every available technique in their pursuit. One might in fact attempt a provisional conclusion at this stage, that the world of social policy, far from displaying the strictly instrumental, means-ends relationships that are found in the more technological worlds of engineering and even medicine is beyond a certain point irreducibly expressive in two distinct respects. The first is that programmes, objectives, far from being determined on a matter of fact basis of what is practically possible have also a social component as expressive symbols of the values of wider society, a society of which scientists themselves are part. These values may be confused, contradictory and hotly disputed: the very uncertainty of practice amply illustrates this. It may be that they should be refined and made more consistent through debate. But nothing can alter the fact that this debate is essentially moral in nature, and one in which science as such can have a part only insofar as it can comment on the practical feasibility or otherwise of particular choices. And the second respect is that in which attitudes to resources, including attitudes to information, testify to the social and expressive nature of ends in being themselves social and expressive. Purely instrumental ways of dealing with other human beings are regarded with suspicion. Here it may be that technological development may itself make inroads on this tradition, as it did in medicine, to an extent at which we cannot even guess. But it is difficult to believe that technological development could transform the whole realm of social policy into one of pure instrumentality. Much more likely seems a shifting of boundaries in the direction of admitting new technologies into such areas as the treatment of delinquency coupled with, and this is of infinitely greater importance, a much more explicit recognition of the grounds on which boundaries are established.

This is all very tentative indeed. But there is enough certainty about it to raise the question of why, social life being after all *social* life in respect of both ends and means, there should be such pressure to replace it by the instrumental relationships of science. One obvious answer is, again, that it is the function of science to replace hunch by knowledge. But the facts of social and moral life are after all facts, they *are* knowledge, and they are knowledge that, although their business if they are anyone's, some social scientists do not seem to want to know about. And certainly a statement of the scientific ethic goes no distance in explaining the enthusiasm with which these scientists pursue this goal. I think we can find some guidance in considering one aspect of the virtuoso role as yet undiscussed, the element of social distance that is involved in any virtuoso activity. I shall suggest in the following chapter that in the pursuit of the virtuoso role, in seeking for 'expert' ways of dealing with people, we see what amounts to a flight from the uncertainty, danger and messiness of authentic social relationships, just as in the purely instrumental cast of much social thought we see a flight from the moral basis in terms of which authentic social relationships are conducted. This theme can usefully be introduced by a discussion of a matter very much to the fore in certain welfare professions, specifically correctional work and special education, that of what we mean when we use the term 'treatment' in these occupations.

CHAPTER SIX

The Concept of Treatment in Non-Medical Settings

The nature of the professional task can further be illustrated by examining the use that is regularly made of the word 'treatment' in such contexts as correctional work and special education. Schools for maladjusted children are specifically charged with the task of providing 'treatment': similarly an important body in the correctional world is the Advisory Council on the Treatment of Offenders. The fact that a word with overtones of medical practice is regularly used in non-medical contexts perhaps tells us something of the aspirations of those who deal with offenders or with the educationally handicapped or with the maladjusted, but it remains necessary to find out in what senses it is used by these groups, and in what senses it might be a useful and appropriate word to use. A possible first step is to examine the various uses of the word in frankly medical contexts, and for purposes of comparison with the institutional setting within which the welfare professions are frequently practised it is as well to focus on clinical practice in the setting of a hospital.

A sociological analysis of hospital practice can usefully examine treatment methods according to a number of criteria: the time-dimension or the duration of treatment; the space-dimension or the physical setting of treatment, with which are associated questions about the extent to which treatment takes place via a distinctive technology; social relations between therapist and patient, and social relations within the treatment team.

Time. When does treatment take place? It is of crucial importance in understanding the treatment situation to know whether treatment is seen as occupying only a brief proportion of a patient's career in hospital, or whether it is something that takes up a substantial proportion, being co-extensive in the extreme case with the whole time the patient is in hospital. Thus a surgical operation may take only a matter of a few hours, or even minutes, and so represents only a small part of the time a patient is in hospital. To be sure pre- and post-operative care is part of 'treatment' too, but surgery is nonetheless characterized by the presence of a critical act that is supposed in itself to set in motion the desired changes in the patient's condition, and that makes the surgeon the virtuoso performer par excellence. Something like a critical act is also found on medical wards, i.e. the act of commencing medication, but here the act has a less dramatic quality by virtue of being repeated at regular intervals. A patient receives a *course* of 'treatment'. In psychiatric hospitals, or on the psychiatric wards of the new District General Hospitals such critical acts may take the form of electro-convulsive therapy, or the administration of drugs. However, at least as far as short and medium-stay patients are concerned there tends in psychiatric hospitals to be present an attitude of mind that sees a patient's treatment as commencing the moment he sets foot in the hospital and as being co-extensive with the duration of his stay there. This is particularly likely to be the case where the orientation is explicitly psychotherapeutic, or where the therapeutic community idea has taken hold, or where otherwise the use of medical and surgical techniques is seen as only one of the many types of influence that may be brought to bear on a patient.

Space. Where does treatment take place? It is equally important to distinguish between those contexts where treatment is seen as taking place in only a limited number of locations within the hospital and those where treatment is not so localized. In the extreme case, again, the location of treatment may be seen as co-extensive with the whole organization, so that it may sometimes be said that the hospital, rather than any particular facilities within it, is itself the treatment. The Henderson Hospital is one place where this has been said.

Thus surgical operations are peculiarly localized. This is crucially related to the high degree of technological development that has taken place in surgical practice: unlike the surgery of the nineteenth century it is no longer possible to carry out operations in the ward itself, still less in the patient's home. So a distinction emerges between the theatre and the ward: what goes on in the theatre is one thing, the 'treatment' itself perhaps; what goes on in the ward is a process of preparing the patient for the theatre, or looking after him after he has been there until finally he is discharged. Medical wards are characterized by an enlargement of the area of treatment activity, treatment being given at the bedside. This is related to the more portable nature of medical equipment. Here again, however, it is possible to point to places where treatment is *not* carried on, e.g. the sluices, or a sister's office or the nursing station. The confinement of a patient to bed has the particular effect of defining areas of the ward and of the hospital as neutral ground in respect of treatment. In psychiatric hospitals there may be similarly a room specially set aside for E.C.T. Where, however, a small ward is taken over temporarily this will be closed for everyday ward purposes because it is 'being used for treatment', i.e. the ward at other times is not a treatment area, and other wards at the same time are not treatment areas. In some psychiatric hospitals there may be special 'treatment rooms' set aside for psychotherapy or occupational therapy, and in such hospitals it is common to find patients not only defining what takes place outside these areas as not treatment but, returning to the first criterion, sitting outside the door *waiting for treatment to begin*. Increasingly, however, it is common to find inroads being made on this notion of spatially defined treatment, at least in psychiatry, and in those institutions where it is said that treatment begins the moment a patient crosses the threshold it will perhaps also be said that treatment is not something that is localized in an occupational therapy room or in a doctor's office but is the totality of influences brought to bear on a patient wherever in the institution he may be at any time.

Social relations between treatment team and patient. Is treatment something that is 'done' to or 'given' to a patient, or is it something to which he is himself necessarily obliged to contribute, and perhaps even to play a major part? Specifically, what part is played by the ideas of co-operation and even initiative on the part of the patient? The patient's co-operation in surgery is minimal; as like as not he will be anaesthetized. He is socially neutral, and during an opera-

tion the surgeon's relation to him is descriptively similar to that
of a mechanic towards the car he is repairing.[1] Surgeons do in
fact refer to themselves from time to time jokingly as mechanics
or plumbers. In medicine too the treatment tends to be something
that is *given*,[2] though the fact that the patient is as a rule conscious
presents the possibility of more complex relationships between
the clinician and patient that have been the subject of much discussion. Thus a physician may on the one hand utilize the possibility of a social relationship to the end of treatment, as when it is
felt that a patient needs encouragement, perhaps even reprimand;
on the other it is often felt that this possibility presents dangers
in the form of 'involvement' that may jeopardize the treatment
process, so that a strictly 'professional' relationship becomes the
ideal. Clinical practice has inherited two opposed principles in
this matter. The older tradition, stressing the ideal of detachment,
is expressed in such aphorisms as 'A good nurse doesn't mind
moving', and certainly it is this ethic that is being built into the
conveyor-belt system implied in the concept of 'progressive
patient care'. Here the movement of the patient from person to
person and from ward to ward is dictated entirely by his stage of
recovery. The system is designed strictly as a means of making
the most economic use of human and physical resources. Yet at
the same time partly owing to the impact of psychosomatic
medicine increased attention is being given to the importance of
human relations in medical care and to such matters as the effect
of the ward atmosphere on recovery. The conflict between these
two positions is of course magnified in psychiatry. The loss of
detachment on the part of a therapist presents considerably
greater problems because of the markedly social component of
much psychological illness, yet precisely because of the equally
social component in psychotherapy it is in psychiatry where it is
most difficult to preserve. In long term psychotherapy in particular the treatment setting is such that the development of social
relationships of a kind not easily distinguishable from relationships outside a treatment setting can hardly be avoided, and the

[1] ' "Thank God," remarked a surgeon, "I don't have to talk to my cases. I need
not see anything of them except the affected area. That's why I'm a good surgeon." '
(Cohen, 1964, p. 16.)

[2] 'Nurses . . . have a lot in common with colonial governors, eager to lavish a lifetime on their subjects, give them drains and drugs – always provided there's no
question of actually working *with* the natives.' (Ibid, p. 57.)

theoretical problem becomes one of how to guide a social relationship that has, by definition, elements of spontaneity in its development. Thus the therapist is forced into the position of observing himself in social interaction, something that is not required of the surgeon. It is scarcely possible to conceive of a treatment situation in which the relationship between patient and therapist might become completely spontaneous and yet remain in any accepted sense a treatment relationship, so this polar position is necessarily unoccupied. Yet where, as in psychoanalysis, a patient may be of very high intelligence and have problems no more acute than those of his analyst this extreme is approached, and tales are told of the patient taking over and analysing the analyst.

Social relations within the treatment team. In whom is 'treatment' located? Is it in the hands of an expert, a therapeutic virtuoso who is assisted in a supportive or ancillary capacity by people of lesser therapeutic expertise? Or is it located in a wider group? Until quite recently (the situation is changing, particularly in respect of the anaesthetist's role), the conduct of a surgical operation tended to be shaped by the decisions and actions of a single expert, uniquely qualified to perform the critical act already discussed, and notwithstanding their own expertise in other capacities the role of anaesthetist and theatre sister were seen as supportive or facilitative. On a medical ward, however, the nursing staff might take a much more active part in the 'giving' of treatment insofar as the critical act had been replaced by a series of events, and the relationship between nursing and medical staff subtly changed. But though the source of treatment is now located in a group rather than in an individual it is still possible quite clearly to define who is not a member of this group. The clinical team consists of doctors and nurses, but not of the cleaners or the ladies from the W.V.S. who come round with library books. Yet where the patient is a child, or where the patient's condition is felt to have a psychosomatic component (a consideration that can extend to a surprising number of pathological conditions once one starts thinking this way) even this distinction may nowadays be felt to be arbitrary, and in the children's hospitals, sanatoria, geriatric wards and on the medical wards of some general hospitals attention is now being given to the therapeutic potential of non-clinical staff, of relatives and other visitors and even of other patients. In psychiatric hospitals where exclusive reliance is placed on medication it may be possible to restrict the notion of who is giving treatment to clinical staff only; much more common today, however, is an awareness of the therapeutic potential of anyone with whom the patient comes in contact. In the extreme case where no form of medication is used at all, as at the Henderson Hospital, 'treatment' becomes equivalent to 'influence', and the fact that influence may be exerted from any direction may become the foundation of treatment philosophy. Far from being a therapeutic virtuoso the doctor becomes primus inter pares, the co-ordinator of a therapeutic team that may extend to include the patients themselves, and himself distinguished only by a greater degree of sophistication in interpretation, and by an ultimate clinical responsibility for the outcome of events.

Such an analysis raises the question of which of the two polar extremes, surgery or psychiatry, seems to be more in mind when the word 'treatment' is used in relation to approved schools, or schools for maladjusted children, or borstals, or prisons. Is it supposed that treatment within such institutions will take the form of a critical event or relatively short series of events that will themselves initiate change in a desired direction, or is treatment thought of as a multiplicity of influences and experiences exerted over a much longer period? Secondly, is treatment something localized within the establishment in the form of something equivalent to a treatment room or an operating theatre, or is it thought of as equivalent to the total experience of being present within the institution? Then is treatment seen as something that is 'given' to an inmate, or is it something that will involve the formation of a social relationship with him, and perhaps require co-operation and effort on his part? Finally is this treatment seen as in the hands of a restricted number of experts skilled in relatively esoteric techniques, or is it thought of as being located in a much wider group of people defined by their capacity to exert desirable forms of influence?

To ask one of these questions is virtually to ask them all, for the four criteria are functionally related. The nature of the surgical task, for example, is such that it prescribes not only the need for a specialized locale, but also a certain social structure within the treatment team and a certain relationship with the patient. Conversation with the patient would probably not materially add to the surgeon's stock of useful information, and this consideration perhaps plays its part in the use of general anaesthetics, even where local anaesthetics would be manageable. On the other hand conversation is the very essence of the psychotherapist's activities, and insofar as his expertise consists less in esoteric manipulative skills than in a more sophisticated grasp of a kind of knowledge that is otherwise quite public the possibility of a marked social distance between psychiatrist and non-psychiatrist is by that much reduced, as is the possibility of an entirely impersonal approach to his patient. Similarly while in the matter of the location of treatment the surgeon's skills are exercised in the use of technical equipment that is not to be found in any odd corner, the non-manipulative skills of the psychiatrist do not require specialized locations to anything like the same extent. The question is: which of these total settings most resembles that of practice in the welfare professions?

In respect of the social relationship between therapist and client the tradition in the welfare professions has tended to be emphatically towards the psychiatric end of the continuum. That it is impossible to do anything with or for one's client unless a working social relationship has been established is a commonplace both of penology and of education. In respect of the space and time criteria also there seems to be much in the situation of correctional practice or of special school work that resembles mental hospital psychiatry. Certainly the treatment, whatever it is, is not such that anyone can designate any particular locality within the establishment as where it takes place. Nor can one point to any clearly defined critical acts that will themselves precipitate the outcome of 'rehabilitation' or 'education' or 'reform'. Critical events may and do occur in the careers of clients that seem to exert a quite disproportionate influence on them; the point is that such experiences cannot as a rule be planned for.

But this is to beg the question, for whether there is in the welfare professions any place for critical acts analogous to those of surgery or medicine, and by extension for the virtuoso performer is exactly the point at issue. For notwithstanding the previous paragraph, what seems to be at the back of their minds when many people talk of the treatment of offenders or of maladjusted children is exactly such a form of virtuoso activity. And such a notion would not be entirely without precedent in the history of humanitarian practice. The religious and ethical roots of penal practice, for example, have always tended to encourage a habit of thinking in terms of critical events, of an inmate suddenly 'seeing the light' or undergoing a dramatic experience equivalent to a conversion. Moreover such a notion offers scope for genuinely virtuoso activity: prisons and borstals have chaplains appointed to them, and one form of treatment that is regularly employed in all penal establishments, as in approved schools, an activity that satisfies all the criteria of space, time and social structure associated with the virtuoso role, is the Sunday service. And, the religious tradition apart, the idea of virtuoso intervention corresponds to fairly widespread assumptions about the importance in both correctional work and in education of charismatic individuals, possessed of rare qualities of personal magnetism. A not uncommon problem in correctional establishments is that posed by the newcomer, or the visitor, or the approved school manager who feels sure that by having a few words by himself with a boy, or speaking to an inmate as man to man he can get him on the right lines or otherwise achieve unique results. The corresponding problem in special education is that of the visiting psychotherapist who feels sure that he can personally set to rights problems that have been beyond the powers of the rest of the staff even to accurately diagnose.

In view of this tradition it is not surprising that thoughts should turn from time to time to the possibility of forms of virtuoso therapy that bring about desirable changes in prisoners or borstal boys, or in approved school children, or in maladjusted children by means other than prolonged and intimate contact in daily life. Virtuoso activities have high prestige; general care activities as a rule do not. This consideration affects the attitude to the welfare occupations both of those already in practice and of those outside who would like to feel part of the treatment process but to whom refereeing football matches, supervising meals and getting inmates out of bed have little appeal.

Within the practitioner group these considerations are further complicated by the fact that the very recognition that professional autonomy and status tend to be associated with the possession of esoteric skills may mean that such skills are sought and used as a means of securing autonomy and status, and not because they demonstrably further any specific professional objectives. There are obvious respects in which such penological techniques as social case-work and group counselling not only provide a form of intervention that is morally acceptable but also meet the needs of the staff in other ways. In some borstal establishments there is a clear disposition, on the part of inmates as well as of staff, to look upon group counselling as 'The Treatment', an attempt to establish virtuoso activities that are restricted both in space (special rooms may be set aside for group counselling) and in time (treatment is given on specific evenings in the week).

Outside the professional group there are rather often attempts to talk of the welfare professions as if they could be quickly brought up to date by the use of techniques and skills that are readily available but wilfully neglected. A recent example in the prison and borstal world is provided by the discussion that followed the publication of the A.C.T.O. report (*The Organization of After-care: Report of the Advisory Council on the Treatment of Offenders* H.M.S.O., 1963). One of the main recommendations of this report was the employment of professional social workers both within and outside all prisons and some other penal establishments, with a view to securing continuity in the treatment of offenders. Paragraphs 91 to 94 of this report, however, indicated that such an arrangement was not recommended for borstal institutions, for although:

'Most housemasters are not particularly well equipped by training and experience for after-care functions. Their training deals mainly with the administration of penal institutions and not with social casework. . . .'

it was felt by the advisory council that a borstal housemaster, i.e. an Assistant Governor Class II has a close personal contact with his boys that renders him the most suitable person to deal with after-care agencies outside the borstal:

'The housemaster . . . is, under the governor, responsible not only for the general administration of his house, but also for the personal training and guidance of each of the fifty or more boys comprising it. Thus the basic responsibility for the success of borstal training rests upon his shoulders; he must know each boy and his home background; he must be aware of the outside influences that may have some bearing on the boy's delinquency or affect his attitude to society, and with which the boy may have to contend when he goes out. The housemaster is thus well placed to fulfil as a natural extension of his present training functions the after care functions performed in prison by a specialist social worker. We believe it to be possible and desirable to entrust the main social casework functions in boys' borstals to the housemaster, provided their recruitment and training are revised with these extended duties in mind.'

Thus training in methods of social casework was recommended for Assistant Governors Class II. This provision attracted the following comment from *New Society* on October 17th, 1963:

'More doubtful are the proposals for the training of assistant borstal governors in social work. It would be more logical to have really professional social workers in all borstals and not just in some, and to recognize that assistant governors are junior managers working closely with inmates and staff and train them as such. This would make major retraining on promotion less necessary, obviate role-confusion (and infuriate the Old Guard).'

Similarly Mr. Hugh Klare, writing in the *British Journal of Criminology* (Vol. 4, No. 3, p. 270) argued:

'It might be better to recognize the need for separate client centred case-workers in all Borstals, working in consultation with staff at all levels but especially with inmate-staff centred A.G.s II.'

The remark in parentheses of the *New Society* extract nicely indicates the antagonism with which, in correctional work, the advocates of an entirely 'therapeutic' approach (generally, to the credit of the clinicians within the service, on the part of those not actually in practice) view the existing management in correctional institutions and managerial problems generally. For it is clearly implied that there exists a kind of treatment that can be administered only by 'really professional social workers' and which can be administered separately from the business of running an institution. The A.C.T.O. report recommends the appointment of caseworkers in all prisons because no other grades of staff are specifically charged with welfare responsibilities. The *New Society* note, on the other hand, appears to recommend the appointment of social caseworkers in borstals on quite other grounds, that although a housemaster has day-to-day contact with a boy there is an acknowledged form of expertise in the treatment of offenders that he lacks but which social caseworkers possess. One wonders what this might be?

Certainly there seems to be no longer any general assurance among psychiatrists that forms of intermittent contact not involving the use of surgery or medication have any particularly crucial effect, except where such contact is founded on a quality of personal relationship that is by no means invariably present, and which is not entirely the outcome of training. In their well-known study of Chestnut Lodge Sanatorium, Doctors Stanton and Schwartz indicate that the influence of the 'therapeutic hour' with the psychiatrist was by no means paramount when compared with the influence of nurses, aides and other patients with whom the inmate had contact over the remaining twenty-three hours (Stanton and Schwartz, 1954). In this country the unique potency of a psychotherapeutic interview in an outpatient department once a fortnight is by no means taken for granted, and effort in many places is now focused on more continuous contact by means of an enlarged staff of social workers. Correctional establishments, perhaps due to dissatisfaction with the religious and ethical orientations of former years, perhaps due to a desire to improve the practitioner's status, now seem to have an eye on medical practice as a model. It would be odd if the prison and borstal services were to lose their faith in personal long-term contact and seek a kind of virtuoso professionalism exactly at the point where in many medical fields opinion seems to be stressing the paramount importance of good human relationships. It is difficult, however, to imagine what the content of such an expertise might be, and one would like guidance on what it is envisaged that specialist case-workers might do that only they are qualified to do.

This leads to a second point, one relating to the relationship between treatment activities and administration. The remarks of *New Society* on the A.C.T.O. proposals indicate a common belief that not only are there forms of 'treatment' that can be administered only by 'really professional social workers', but also that this treatment can be administered separately from the business of running an organization. The use of the term 'junior manager' clearly indicates a belief that it is possible to separate the functions of treatment and administration in places like prisons and borstals, and thus betrays an unawareness of the complexity of relationships within any organization where the primary task has to do with people, and where the processes of change are brought about through social relationships. In fact the sharp distinction between administration and treatment is quite spurious. Dr. Terence Morris, in a television interview that followed the publication of the A.C.T.O. report made this same distinction when he suggested that the prison service might take a leaf out of the hospitals' book and create a separate grade of prison administrator so that other members of staff might be left free for treatment duties. This is a fantasy very attractive to liberal academics. Unfortunately the sharp separation of medical and administrative functions on which the argument rests is found only in general hospitals, i.e. in those hospitals that least resemble a correctional establishment. In a psychiatric hospital, or a mental subnormality hospital, or a sanatorium, or indeed in any long stay hospital a hospital administrator will as a rule be very closely involved in the treatment programme, because decisions about purchasing, building, recruitment, the deployment of staff, the use of hospital grounds and a host of other things have direct therapeutic implications. Similarly in a borstal decisions about recreational and educational activities, vocational training, staffing and the composition and size of houses have a direct bearing on 'treatment'. The case for virtuoso treatment roles also fails to come to terms with the crucial question of where in the power structure of an organization a separate grade of therapists is to fit. In a hospital setting the scope given to treatment staff is guaranteed by the fact that they assume ultimate responsibility for the patient's welfare. In a correctional setting this responsibility is assumed by the non-clinical staff, and to introduce a separate role of therapist is therefore an attempt to divorce power from responsibility. For just as an administrative decision has clinical implications, clinical decisions regularly affect the administration of an organization, and the result seems often to be a conflict of interests with an outcome either in the complete undermining of the administrative framework or, more commonly, the subordination of treatment staff to purely residual functions. The conflict may be resolved, as it is in some maladjusted schools and in the psychiatric prison at Grendon Underwood, by appointing a clinician to be the administrative head, but this seems as often as not to result in his becoming sharply aware that in an institutional setting treatment is largely carried out in terms of administrative decisions.

The argument is not that there can never be a place for virtuoso intervention in the non-medical fields that are being considered, indeed this would be to ignore the extent to which in medicine itself the appearance of an authentic technology has repeatedly altered the nature of the therapeutic process. For medicine has developed equally in opposite directions, and if at the present time the importance of the social factor in therapy is being recognized it is also the case that in such fields as the treatment of tuberculosis the appearance of chemotherapy has reduced the need for a specially planned therapeutic regime within the hospital. So we have no reason to suppose that technological developments of the kind that were discussed in Chapter III might not materially alter both the nature of the task in some of the welfare professions and the structure of the organizations within which they are performed. The point is that notwithstanding widespread assumptions to the contrary this stage has not yet been reached. There exists so far no manifestly effective virtuoso technique for reforming borstal boys or relieving the maladjusted. Until such a technique appears the case for introducing such personnel as social caseworkers into positions where they control events within the organization seems to rest on a complete disregard of what standards of performance are in fact required of virtuoso decision makers, and are forthcoming, in organizations conducted on virtuoso lines.

The notion of expertise, and it is generally agreed that the inmates of borstals, special schools and mental hospitals need 'expert' attention, almost automatically suggests virtuoso activity. The image of the surgeon, the scientist, the technologist springs to mind – highly trained personnel practising esoteric skills against a background of non-virtuosi. And the virtuoso performer is a figure of immense prestige and glamour. It is in principle not improbable, then, that there might be a temptation to carry over this model of professional activity into contexts where it is not appropriate, if only at the moment. Because we want the best for our clients there may be a tendency to postulate esoteric knowledge and skills where none exist. Or to look for them in the wrong direction. The case for group counselling and social casework, individual and group psychotherapy is not, I think, that they are effective in bringing about demonstrable results, for we have no evidence that they are. The case for all these things is that they represent what we at the moment regard as the morally acceptable limits to which we are prepared to go in dealing with people who have not requested our intervention. If we, that is either the practitioners or the interested members of society looking on, really want to put the welfare professions on a 'scientific' basis then we should be looking in other directions entirely, to the possibilities of aversion therapy or sleep learning, and that we are not considering these possibilities is perhaps a measure of the extent to which our concern to reshape these professions on a scientific basis stems less from any particular concern with effectiveness than from a desire to have them display the opportunities for social differentiation that are found in the virtuoso professions. The role of the virtuoso performer is one that is admired and well understood by the interested public; the 'general care' roles (for want of a better term) that are found in the welfare professions are not so generally admired, nor understood, nor do they attract theoretical interest.

To those who are in a position to give their minds to this matter the kinds of thing done in special schools and borstals suggest a form of post-humanitarian provision that is out of step with the present day. They do not attract the ambitious for they do not display the performance criteria by which excellence could be demonstrated. They do not attract the scientifically curious, for notwithstanding the talk of 'experiment' that is so common in penology and education the attitude to technical possibilities is distinctly suspicious. They do not even attract people with particularly tidy minds because they are as selective in the use of information as they are in the use of techniques. It is certain that these are bad habits, and that the welfare professions are going to have to change. But at the end of the day it may be that the possibilities of change are not limitless, that the elements of ideal, faith and technical restraint are still with us because this is what the welfare professions are *about*.

This is nowhere more apparent than in the use that has come to be made of the idea of the 'therapeutic community'. Here we have an idea that could quite easily be understood purely as the exploitation of the properties of social life to entirely instrumental ends: an ingenious resolution of the traditional distinction between 'gemeinschaft', and 'gesellschaft', 'community' and 'association' (MacIver, 1937). The specifically medical origins of the concept would suggest this. These are perhaps to be traced to the discovery in 1904 by two Parisian psychiatrists that in the Saltpetriere hospital those patients who occupied beds on a large public ward seemed in better mental and physical health than the private patients, or perhaps to the discovery in the following year by Dr. K. J. Pratt of Boston that tubercular patients seemed to benefit physically from receiving instruction in groups. But it is clear that one might view the therapeutic community idea from quite another standpoint, as the reappearance in a clinical setting of the much older tradition of community living associated with actual Utopianism. Professor Armytage does in fact give attention to the therapeutic community movement in his study of the history of Utopianism (Armytage, 1961). Such a standpoint helps to make more intelligible the attitudes and activities of staff who choose to work on this basis, and not merely in the prison and borstal service either where one might expect the clinical origins of the idea to be less apparent but also in such a place as the Henderson Hospital where these activities take place under medical auspices. One difficulty regularly encountered is that of trying to get a precise statement about the way therapeutic community treatment, along with a host of other activities including group counselling, is supposed to work. In 1954 I joined the staff of the Henderson Hospital, then the Belmont Hospital Social Rehabilitation Unit, as a research worker, and as I was entirely new to the world of welfare practice this question still seemed a reasonable one to ask. Rightly or wrongly I expected that a clear statement would be forthcoming, and in 'medical', probably psychodynamic terms. In the event it proved singularly difficult to get a rationale of therapy at all. No one seemed at all sure what it was in the experience to which a patient was exposed that was thought to be doing him good, or why. This degree of uncertainty contrasted with the considerable clarity on the part of the staff about the ways in which a community environment assisted *diagnosis*. These were as follows:

In the first place as the patients were there because of difficulties with other people rather than because of intra-psychic delusions and the like a 'real life' situation offered peculiar advantages as these difficulties manifested themselves on the spot. The therapist did not have to be told what was wrong: he could see for himself. Secondly, as the therapeutic process was continuous, and not confined to a single interview at intervals of time, concealment of symptoms was impossible. Any and everything could be and was discussed in the therapeutic groups or at the early morning meetings when the whole community assembled in one room.

This greater clarity about diagnostic processes no doubt reflected to some extent the balance of forces in psychodynamic theory generally. It is still easier to say what is wrong with a patient than to say what to do about it. There were other reasons, however, that were peculiar to this one place. It was possible to see the diagnostic advantages of the Unit at work. A discovery, an item of knowledge gained, was a discrete event that claimed attention, and in the Unit, where everything took place in public, such revelations tended to be dramatic. 'Treatment' on the other hand was not an event but a process, and a long term one at that. There were no startling and sudden 'cures', and few changes for the better that could with any confidence be related to any specific cause, and it was difficult to say whether and in what way any particular patient had benefited, though many patients were quite sure that they had. Thus there were good reasons why staff of the Unit were tentative about explaining the treatment. If pressed, however, they might make one or other of the following suggestions:

Thus from time to time one encountered a belief that the catharsis that accompanied the revelation of a patient's difficulties was particularly beneficial when these revelations were more or less public. Now this belief is not, of course, confined to psychotherapists. There is a long tradition in England, religious in origin, of public examination and confession, and the community setting made it possible to exploit the value set on these activities. An explicit comparison was sometimes made by members of the staff with the activities of the Oxford Group between the wars. Secondly, at a more didactic level, the community was felt to provide a large reservoir of personal experience which might be used to instruct a patient. It was not supposed that patients might provide profound insights of a psychoanalytic kind, but rather that in a community of a hundred people a patient might reasonably expect to find someone with a problem similar to his own. Furthermore a patient might be more ready to listen to someone with first-hand experience than to someone whose knowledge must necessarily be academic much of the time. Again, there was nothing specifically medical about processes such as this. They go on all the time, everywhere. Finally it was sometimes suggested that as a consequence of these two experiences a patient, by developing a 'transference to the group' or to the community at large, would in fact be taking the first steps in socialization or the development of fellow-feeling, a quality in which many of the patients were startlingly deficient. But if this was 'transference' then certainly it had the advantage of not being followed by complications such as negative transference and the need for a weaning period such as are found in two-person psychotherapeutic relationships which the word transference usually suggests. There was no reason, in fact, why such relationships should not have been regarded as 'normal social relationships', and in fact patients no doubt occasionally kept in touch with each other afterwards. There was no reason why they should not.

In none of these respects did the social processes within the Unit differ very much from those of everyday social life. Yet these were no more than tentative suggestions about what was going on. There was one conviction about treatment beside which these considerations were seen as of minor importance, a conviction that was often expressed and in terms that were remarkably non-medical in nature. This was that whatever else a patient might do, unless he participated fully in the life of the community he would not derive maximum benefit from his stay there. This was very often heard. And as the culture of the Unit was in many ways different from that of the outside world, for example in the encouragement given to public discussion of highly personal matters, to participate fully in this life involved a definite decision to have done with old values and to adopt new ones, a decision often accompanied by a degree of personal crisis. The decision to adopt these new values was spoken of as 'coming into treatment', and there was a widespread assumption that once a patient had come into treatment this in itself would set him on the road to recovery. Indeed on occasion the fact of 'coming into treatment' was spoken of as if it was itself equivalent to recovery.

Now the most striking thing about these phenomena was the extent to which they resembled the processes of conversion to a religion or to a political creed. There was nothing conspicuously medical about them. Similarly the most striking thing about the belief in the value of personal involvement was its familiarity. It is exactly the same kind of thing that gets said to new boys in boarding schools and to new recruits in the army. In both these environments the newcomer is required to adopt new and often highly unusual values before he can begin to 'feel at home'. And having eventually accepted these values he gains, in both cases, the support that comes from membership of a restricted society.

This line of thinking brings in question common assumptions about the distinctiveness of the clinical situation. Generally speaking we expect the things that happen in hospitals to be in significant respects different from those in other organizations. It is not so much that we expect the presence of shining instruments, the atmosphere of clinical sterility and so on, though these are important. It is rather that we expect a certain approach, an attitude that is peculiar to medical contexts, and this is not found in other places where people are being 'done good to'. This is an attitude of detachment, of precision and of skill. We expect a high degree of consciousness on the part of staff. We expect, in short, 'expertise'. Certainly the Unit's patients expected these things when they arrived. They were, of course, disappointed, and it was a feature of the early stages of every patient's career that he had to accept that this was 'not that kind of hospital'. To understand the Unit it was necessary to abandon expectations about what would constitute a therapeutic process. It eventually proved more useful to think of it not so much as a new departure in medicine but as a reappearance under medical auspices of a traditional use of community life as a means of promoting well-being. The therapeutic community, on this line of thinking, has precedents not only in schools and in the army, but perhaps most explicitly in monastic life, and in many Utopian communities that have been founded at various times. Looking back on this experience I do not feel that the resemblance to a religious community was accidental – a thought that has occurred to people who have undergone other kinds of experience such as T-groups and other

106

forms of sensitivity training.

This is to view the therapeutic community idea from the standpoint of a sociologist rather than of a clinician. Such a standpoint forces us to question the idea that there is something characteristic of 'treatment' that makes it different from 'education', 'rehabilitation' or even 'salvation'. The actual activities of hospitals, prisons, schools and religious communities are perhaps not qualitatively different, but are defined by the context in which they occur. Precisely the same activity may be psychotherapy if carried on in a hospital, education if carried on in a school, training or rehabilitation if carried on in a prison or borstal. The occurence in our society of specialized institutions at the interstices between two or more professions underlines this point. Thus we have schools for maladjusted children ('treatment' or 'education'?); approved schools ('education' or 'reform'?); and penal establishments where they practise a form of group psychotherapy ('reform' or 'treatment'?). It is misleading, in fact, to think in such terms as 'treatment' or 'education', which refer not to an activity but to a professional affiliation, more useful to think in purely descriptive terms of promoting change in people in directions that are felt to be desirable. In this way the problem is brought near enough for inspection and loses some of its awe. We are thus prepared to find ways in which the activities of clinicians, at least of psychiatrists, resemble those of other professional persons perhaps more than we expected.

It is possible, for example, to accept the difficulty and perhaps impossibility of standardizing the therapeutic process in institutional treatment as if it were an aspirin because every institution is, precisely because it is a community, unique. Whether or not there is some kind of instrumental activity such as medication or surgery going on is of course going to make a difference, but this is not something that much concerns people who work in correctional institutions or in schools. For example the treatment experience in an institution varies through time. Like all human societies the Unit had its ups and downs. With each change of personnel the nature of the experience changed. An intake of aggressive and anti-social patients profoundly changed the mood of the place, and this in turn affected what happened to other patients. Variations in the discharge rate suggested that a change in the medical staff was invariably accompanied by some degree of social disturbance (Rapoport, 1956, 1960). A practical consequence of these fluctuations was that the outcome of a patient's stay might well be determined by the particular period in which he 'received treatment'.

Now it is obviously in nobody's interest when an institution is brought near collapse through no control having been exercised over its intake. Yet to regard this lack of standardization as a defect would be to avoid the obvious fact that uniqueness and a tendency to change are a feature of every community. It was no idle claim that the Unit provided a 'real life' situation. The Unit was not *like* a real community; it was not some kind of model; it *was* a community with all that this implied. Nor, for the same reason, was it an idle claim that the treatment was continuous, for people did influence one another by the mere fact of living together. To put the matter another way, and the staff of the Unit were very explicit about this, the treatment was not something a patient received within the Unit, it *was* the Unit. This was no mere slogan. It was recognition of what must be the case in any institutional setting where no forms of medication or surgery or any similar instrumental intervention takes place. For because the Unit was 'real life' its influence was, though variable and unpredictable, extremely powerful. The effect of living full-time in the community was considered more potent as a factor in changing people than any specific psychotherapeutic procedures, necessarily brief and intermittent could ever have been.

It is difficult to escape the conclusion that this must necessarily be the case in any organization operating on a similar basis. We have no choice in the matter. The welfare professions are those that have little in the way of distinctive, non-social forms of intervention to make use of. Here, therefore, the community therapy approach, i.e. the analysis and if possible control of the forces produced by an institutional setting becomes not only useful but mandatory. To put the matter another way to 'establish' a therapeutic community involves not the bringing into being of something that was not there before, but recognition of and a readiness to exploit what is in any case going to happen.

This, of course, immediately brings in question the practice of implicity defining 'treatment' (or 'education', or 'rehabilitation') as *that which the staff provides,* and so to the problem of what role the professional staff are going to play. For they are required to be responsible for a process over which they can have only limited *control*. This is no doubt something that worries the man in charge more than anyone, but it ought to concern any teacher, any social worker, any psychologist or any psychiatrist who chooses to work in an institutional setting. It certainly worries borstal housemasters, no doubt because they have no conspicuous expertise to deceive themselves with.

Yet even when this element of randomness has been recognized some forms of control are obviously possible and necessary. Control is, of course, present in the initial planning of organizations, in decisions about what time and space to allocate to what activities. In this connection, however, some have envisaged a completely 'spontaneous' growth, with patients as active as the staff in the forming of crucial initial decisions. Such ideas are, I think, illusory, mainly because the staff are never in a position to delegate entire responsibility to patients, being inevitably bound by external obligations derived from professional standards of conduct or the law of the land. Thus a doctor must ensure that a patient's physical or mental well-being is not jeopardized; the headmaster of an approved school is not in a legal position to permit a child to leave the school at will. However high a value is placed upon self-expression or, as it was called in the Unit 'acting out' this cannot be allowed to proceed to a point where lives are endangered, or, beyond a certain point, the property of the neighbours. This is to draw attention again to the environmental considerations that institutional activities have to defer to, but this is an area in which the need for control is clearly implied. And control of this sort will clearly have to take place after the initial stage as well.

These thoughts help to pinpoint the highly ambiguous feelings that professional people may sometimes have about control, for control means two quite different things. Control of a treatment process is a highly professional matter, and one that is properly the concern of a virtuoso. The *social* control of an organization is a matter of mere administration, a matter of order that it is difficult to see has much to do with the training that was received particularly by clinical staff. It is perhaps this feeling that underlies the high value that is often placed on being *non-directive*. Thus in the Unit there was apparently little or no attempt actually to precipitate events; the only acceptable form of staff intervention was in the *interpretation* of events as they happened. But this practice served two quite distinct purposes, one acknowledged and the other, I think, not. On the one hand, and this was the purpose to which the staff of the Unit directed attention, the practice served as a means of deepening a patient's understanding of himself and how he affected others. On the other it served as a means of communicating the unexpressed values of the place, indicating quite clearly just what forms of behaviour the institution could tolerate and what it could not. To a far higher degree than was formally recognized responses were patterned, and well understood. When a patient absented himself from a therapeutic group, or left a meeting slamming the door this might be a spontaneous expression of tension but was more likely to be a known means of getting one's problems talked about – a request for help. When staff members said of a patient that he 'did not want treatment' this tended to mean that the patient's behaviour was becoming more than the institution could cope with, and was accepted as such. Sometimes unacceptable forms of behaviour might be defined in advance as indicating that the patient 'did not want treatment'. Thus, on one occasion, a staff member suggested that an alcoholic patient be confined to the hospital precincts for a month so that if he did go out and get drunk 'it will mean that he doesn't want treatment'.

In this way, notwithstanding a formal ethos of permissiveness, the problem of order was fully acknowledged. For this purpose the staff of the Unit made use of the essentially social sanctions of praise, reprimand, punishment, reward, and ultimately expulsion. From the clinical standpoint, from almost any *professional* standpoint the use of such techniques may seem odd. It is probably not to do this kind of thing that a man sets out to become a clinician. (Teachers, however, are quite used to this. The view that a school is a society in miniature has never been seriously questioned). But from the standpoint that sees a hospital or a school or a borstal as subject to the conditions that govern any organization they are unavoidable. That the use of such techniques was customarily disguised in technical language indicates only that clinicians and others may sometimes fail to appreciate the implications of what they are doing. In the welfare professions any relationship is a social relationship; in an institutional setting the fact is only magnified.

CHAPTER SEVEN

Government and Training in the Welfare Professions

In previous chapters two themes have appeared repeatedly. One is that notwithstanding the welfare practitioner's desire for professional autonomy the welfare professions are rooted in the values of wider society, and are therefore matters in which society will remain vitally interested. The second is that notwithstanding the search for distinctive professional skills that will secure the practitioner expert status there can be no complete withdrawal from the essentially social nature of welfare practice. These considerations are crucial to any assessment of the political situation of the welfare practitioner.

The situation of the welfare professions seems to be marked by forms of government and control that are quite unlike those of the virtuoso professions. These are occupations that in certain crucial respects, of which even the setting of professional objectives is one, are subject to a degree of control on the part of people not actually belonging to them. Limited goals may appear to be set, but it is not often the practitioner who sets them. If Rule One is properly to be considered a legitimate professional objective it is still significant that it is not an objective that the governor grades of the prison and borstal service decided on after due consideration but one that was given them by people who were not themselves practitioners. In this connection it is illuminating to compare the varying relations of medical practitioners to the Ministry of Health and of teachers and members of the prison service to the Department of Education and Science and the Home Office. Little genuine possibility of extra-professional direction exists in those occupations that have developed specialized skills and esoteric procedures, and where a manifest disaster criterion exists, indeed it is only in the last few years that the medical profession has been subject to any degree of public scrutiny at all. Teaching and penal policy on the other hand are subject to a considerable degree of extra-professional direction, not only from central and local government but also from academic bodies, criminologists and educationists, who have no necessary day to day contact with the professional scene.

To some extent this situation is to be explained in terms of the structure of power in a society which still bears strong evidence of an aristocratic past. Thus with the incursion of expert and esoteric knowledge into such fields as industry, economics, health and even warfare there remain each year progressively fewer fields left for the active intervention of that traditional representative of the ruling class, the uninvolved amateur. Much has been written on amateur government in recent years, and the principle has come in for a lot of well deserved criticism.[1] What has not been pointed out so far is that amateur rule can be attacked and undermined only to reappear elsewhere, perhaps even among the ranks of the attackers.

Thus the locus of amateur direction in such matters as education and penology now seems to be among the ranks of journalists and television personalities, and above all within the universities. This is the argument of this final chapter.

It seems to be extra-professional direction that teachers and penologists have in mind when they complain of their lack of 'professional' status. For many years teachers and prison officials have felt that there are simply too many people ready to tell them what to do.[2] Now in the general distrust of non-professional direction the trainer himself does not escape criticism. Hence the central problem in professional training in this area is perhaps that of confidence between the students and those who teach them, a feeling on the part of students that their teachers will take

---

[1] Though the unique virtues of amateurism were defended as recently as 1960. (Balniel, 1960).

[2] Mr. Sewell Stokes has written: 'My personal view of the prison system, arrived at after an investigation during which I deliberately went out of my way to criticize the established order that I might learn what its supporters had to say in its defence ended by convincing me that prisons could be more easily, and possibly more successfully, run if less attention were paid to the advice given by outsiders.' (Stokes 1960.)

seriously the problems of practice, will not condescend, will not strike poses and will in general not bamboozle them. Yet in fact the task of training is regularly marked by the absence of such confidence. When I began teaching at the Prison Staff College four years ago I soon became aware of a well established tradition that what was taught there was 'ivory towered', 'out of touch with the job', and so on. Similar feelings, perhaps mixed in this case with a degree of actual suspicion, seemed to be entertained towards the Prison Department of the Home Office, and an uneasy mixture of respect and irritation was and still is commonly felt for such bodies as the Howard League for Penal Reform, for university departments of criminology, and for the many politicians, journalists and others who take an active interest in penal policy. Attitudes to the trainers were inextricably mixed with attitudes towards those who formally or informally influenced penal policy: the problem of training was part of the problem of government.

But I was not encountering this phenomenon for the first time. My awareness of this mood was assisted by my previous experiences as a teacher. It seems that every teacher has his repertoire of anecdotes to illustrate the ineptitude of the lecturers at his training college or department of education. Such anecdotes centre on the themes of actual incompetence in the presence of a class, or the irrelevance to practice of lecture material, or its downright untruth – particularly in connection with problems of discipline – or prevarication in the face of awkward questions. It is certain that tales of this kind get told for the fun of it, and that the truth has no doubt been licked into shape in many instances. Yet it would be facile to dismiss such tales as entirely without foundation, for folklore at the very least assesment does provide information about attitudes, and one wonders why attitudes should be so regularly negative. And it is worth noting that this complex of attitudes on the part of teachers is not in fact confined to those who taught them to be teachers. As with prison staffs the themes of training and government go hand in hand. So opinion seems often to be equally disrespectful to those other inhabitants of the educational world, the educational administrators, the educational psychologists, the inspectors, perhaps most of all to those members of local authorities, journalists and other interested parties who assume the title of 'educationist'. Teachers, perhaps especially non-graduate teachers, often seem to feel that there are too many people higher in the social and professional hierarchies telling them how to do their jobs without any apparent real awareness of what that job is.

Now if training in these two professions really is as irrelevant to the working situation as many would claim, if comment really is as ill-informed, then we have reason to be worried. Even if there is no substance in these charges the very attitudes they reveal are sufficient to deserve examination. Neither of these matters can usefully be explored without some examination of a neglected area of human experience: the exact difference between doing a job and talking about it, thinking about it, doing research on it. What, to use the most familiar but at the same time the crudest categories, is the relationship between 'involvement' and 'detachment'? Why, to state the matter empirically, is it so difficult to convey the flavour of actuality that it is a commonplace of so many practitioners that the only way to learn is on the job?

An obvious first step is to examine the communication problem – the difficulty of 'keeping in touch'. For in the act of taking up an appointment as trainer the practitioner is obviously going to be separated immediately from the discipline he is teaching, and this will become more apparent as time goes on.

Two solutions have been found to this problem. One is the short tour of duty as in the army. Military education authorities will state frankly that a long spell of teaching duties means that an officer is all too soon talking about situations that have long ceased to exist. Lectures have to be related to actuality (the existence of a manifest disaster factor in warfare is relevant here) and therefore periodically revised in the light of experience. The prison and borstal service has adopted this solution for those of its teaching staff who come from within the service. Assistant governors seconded to the staff college spend an average of three years in post. The second solution is that found in social work and casework training, and in the training of doctors. This is the simultaneous maintenance of a case load by the trainer himself.

It seems to be only in the training of teachers that the trainer, on being appointed a lecturer in a training college or a department of education, withdraws from practice for ever. In some respects school teaching is the type case of the welfare professions, and it is therefore useful to consider what would be the implications of these arrangements if they were introduced into teacher training. On the one hand we might see the appointment of practising teachers as lecturers in universities and colleges of education for periods of, say, up to five years; on the other the appointment of lecturers for perhaps longer periods, but only on a part-time basis, so that perhaps half the week was spent in school. Supposing the communication problem to be a real one, that teacher trainers do get progressively out of touch with practice, then these are two ways in which the problem might be solved. Either of them would involve financial arrangements between universities and local authorities but this, one supposes, would not be difficult to arrange. Even the salary differential might not present an insuperable problem if there was a general determination to improve the standard of performance. Yet neither of these arrangements, of course, is found. One wonders why. The feeling that teacher training bears insufficient relation to practice is sufficiently widespread for it to be unlikely that there is no truth in it at all, yet a solution that is both familiar and feasible is not even tried. This suggests that there are other factors involved. If the problem is simply one of communication then the solution is relatively simple. If the solution is not adopted then one can only conclude that this must not be the problem, or at least the basic problem.

And in fact it probably is not. It is worth while reflecting, for example, that the separation of theory and practice, far from being an unfortunate but unavoidable fact of life, has frequently been actually advocated. One set of arguments centres on the contrasting ideas of 'involvement' and 'detachment'. The need for detachment in the sense of not being absorbed by the social aspects of a professional situation is of course a commonplace of the welfare professions, indeed it seems to be precisely this detachment that is thought to distinguish a professional from a social relationship. One good reason for this is, of course, the protection of the practitioner. The busy, matter of fact manner of the nurse, to which objections are now being raised (see above, Chapter VI), was encouraged in the past precisely because it protected her from the emotional impact of distressing experiences. For the same reason nurses were frequently moved from ward to ward: 'A good nurse doesn't mind moving'. A similar arrangement has been common in the posting of police officers: policemen were moved frequently specifically to prevent the formation of relationships that might interfere with the proper performance of the job. Yet in both these occupations the practice has been questioned, and in both cases on the grounds that neither the short-stay nurse nor the short-stay policeman are ever likely to be in a position where they really know their clients. On the other hand the virtues of detachment have never been stressed in the teaching profession, which perhaps reflects a greater readiness in the educational world to recognize the relationship between practitioner and client as a social one. The Mr. Chips of the teaching profession have been highly thought of, the transitory careerist suspected. (This ethic of commitment to the organization may have played its part in discouraging the ambitious from the teaching profession. On the other hand it has had the curious result that with the present emphasis on human relations in institutional care the schools find themselves unexpectedly in advance of the rest of the field. Much of the discussion that is currently taking place around the concept of the therapeutic community reflects arguments that have been used by headmasters since the days of Thomas Arnold.)

Much hinges in this discussion on the precise force of the word 'know' when we speak of 'knowing' the client, for 'true knowledge' can be claimed by the advocates of detachment and involvement equally, though the word has a different meaning in each case. There is an epistemological component to each position. Thus the argument for detachment as a means of protection merges into an argument for detachment as a means of preserving insights unclouded. The epistemological argument, one that in fact absorbs the argument of self-protection, is expressed in a host of familiar dicta from the statement that the spectator sees most of the game to Wordsworth's famous definition of poetry as emotion recollected in tranquillity. These ideas are common currency in Britain, and form part of the intellectual climate in which most of us grow up. Much of the argument for separating the study of Education from the practice of teaching, and the study of Criminology from the practice of penal adminsitration and probation work is precisely that it is felt that practice is too much a matter of rough and tumble to permit a clear thought. For this reason we staff our university departments of education and similar training organizations with non-practitioners. And there is much sense in this. The practice accords, moreover, with well established ideas about the place and function of higher education, with the organization of university activities and their relation to practice, and with common views about the proper relationship of universities to the outside world. In the first place universities are traditionally places where 'pure' research goes on, research that is to be 'applied' if at all, in quite other places. (The distinction between 'pure' and 'applied' knowledge is strikingly similar to that between detachment and involvement.) The natural scientist, arguing by analogy from the laboratory world, would no doubt find the argument for an academic study of education, or for an academic study of penal problems entirely convincing, and such views are in turn congruent with the idea that as teaching institutions universities have the task of preparing people for 'life', the dichotomy between the undergraduate years and 'life' being yet another manifestation of the same basic dualism.

Theory and practice, detachment and involvement, pure science and applied science, university and life. To these may be added yet a fifth common dichotomy, the accepted antithesis between thought and action. In some ways this is the crucial one, for it is in terms of this dichotomy that the philosophical basis of higher education in this country seems to have been originally worked out. We owe our ideas on the subject of higher education, just as we owe many features of our political system with which higher education is not unconnected, to Plato. In the Platonic scheme the importance of detachment rests squarely on its being the prerequisite of sound thinking. The basis of Platonic epistemology seems to have rested on his insights into the nature of mathematical concepts. Thus the propositions of geometry are not empirical. The triangles of which the theorems of Pythagoras and Euclid are true are not the triangles that appear in the textbook, for however carefully drawn these must be imperfect. The triangles to which the theorems refer are in fact *ideal*, and in this sense only the ideal is truly real.

This insight has obvious implications for the social ordering of scholarship, for only the man who has withdrawn himself from day to day life, a life symbolized by the approximate triangles that appear in the textbook, is therefore in a position to appreciate true reality. The Platonic theory of knowledge is therefore immensely attractive to people of aristocratic tastes, and one supposes that there has always existed a temptation to transfer an approach that is certainly fruitful in mathematics to areas where it may not be so appropriate. In education, for example, it would seem to follow that while a teacher may know about teaching, only outside the school is one in a position to think about Education – and the further outside the better. Similarly that while a probation officer or prison administrator may spend the whole of his working life dealing with criminals his greatest contribution to exact knowledge must be less than that of the academic commentator who attempts to formulate an ultimate definition of 'Crime'. It is a logical consequence of Platonic epistemology that thought is best carried out by those furthest from the world of action. For a certain range of occupations – those lacking technologies whose mastery is fundamental to practice – the idea accordingly persists that the crucial investigations are carried out not in the classroom but in the study, not by the practitioner but by the theorist. It is a further consequence that within this range there must necessarily be two quite different groups of people involved, not merely teachers but also Educationists, not only prison and borstal staffs but also Criminologists, and it is yet a further consequence that the activities of the former must be subordinated to the activities of the latter. For thought, it is supposed, must precede action; a mastery of theory is fundamental to successful practice. Hence a state of affairs where it may be supposed that the crucial component of teacher training is the development of an insight into 'the nature of education', or that the training of prison staffs and probation officers, and even the teaching of undergraduate students of criminology must be based on an examination, however inconclusive, of the *meaning* of 'Crime'. Hence, moreover, the temptation that faces all academics who find themselves involved in applied fields to argue that the basis of training in social work, or administration, or management, must be a grounding in experimental psychology, or theoretical sociology, or economics, or whatever it is that they are accustomed to teaching to undergraduates.

Now it is certain that there are many areas of education and criminological research that the working practitioner can never have the time or the resources to investigate. It is also certain that every practitioner benefits from the opportunity to get away from his job from time to time, to stand back and see what he is doing. It is equally sure that general goals have to be discussed if the practitioner is to have any real idea of what he is up to. It is by no means clear, however, that the practice of teaching is uniquely based on an insight into 'the nature of education', or that to be a borstal housemaster it is necessary to know all about 'Crime', or that for either it is essential to know a great deal about, respectively, child psychology or academic criminology. For to suppose this is to betray an ignorance of an important fact about professional practice, the extent to which daily activities are neutral in respect of such knowledge, and even in respect of ultimate objectives.

It is useful to consider the question of objectives first. The discussion of practice by those who are not themselves practitioners very often exhibits a characteristic distortion of perception as follows: there arises a belief that actions taken in the conduct of professional life are always taken in deference to ultimate goals. It is easy to see how the fallacy arises. The Platonic method is essentially one of meditation on words. Thus, the purpose of schools is to educate, therefore the teacher, whilst he is on the premises, is educating; prisons and borstals are for rehabilitation and reform, therefore prison and borstal staffs are rehabilitating and reforming all the time (or should be). It would be good if this were so, if prisons really were carefully designed instruments oriented to the single goal of rehabilitation, if schools were delicately arranged for the sole purpose of educating children. Or it might not. For one reason why they are not these things is that they are also communities, and therefore multi-purpose organizations that necessarily serve ends and satisfy values quite other than those implied in any statement of formal objectives. The actions of the practitioner are often taken in deference to considerations quite other than those of 'treatment' or 'education'. In practice an approved school housemaster is as concerned with seeing that beds are properly made, lavatories kept clean and hobby materials properly looked after as he is with 'treatment'. And this not because he is authoritarian, obsessional, second rate and so forth, but because unless these things are done the organization ceases to be a tolerable place to live in. Similarly a teacher necessarily spends much of his time checking pencils, establishing procedures for ventilating rooms, seeing that children do not run into each other in the corridors and so on. It may be objected that these things have nothing to do with education, and that strictly speaking the teacher should not have to do them. The fact remains that if children are educated in schools then at least some of these things have to be done.

It may be argued on the other hand that these considerations are also aspects of education, that schools are miniature societies and that an important aspect of education is learning how to live with one's fellows. This may be so, but to make this claim is substantially to alter the use of the word 'education' (or analogously in the correctional world 'treatment'), and by using the term to rationalize existing procedures to arrive at a position where 'education' is no longer defined as an objective of one's procedures but as a description of those procedures and of the actualities of institutional life. This leads quickly to the position that whatever happens in the organization is education (or treatment). And to the average teacher or housemaster the information that while checking a bath list or giving out table-tennis balls he is engaging in something altogether more elaborate and ambitious may come as a surprise. It may cheer him up. No doubt that is the intention. But it may on the other hand suggest to him that the theorists are merely wishing to assure themselves that the reality of practice corresponds to the image they have created of it.

It is at this point that one begins to get some idea of why the practitioner so often feels that his training taught him nothing, for considerations of this kind are only rarely acknowledged at the training stage. Typically they are dismissed as trivia that can be learned on the job. Even mental hospital psychiatrists seem to come to their task relatively ill-prepared for the realities of the working situation. Encouraged to believe that all decisions can be and will be taken on clinical grounds they may find that some courses of action, however desirable, are precluded because the welfare of other patients would be threatened, because special treatment tends to be interpreted as favouritism, because to introduce new therapeutic procedures may be to invite resistance from the entire structure of rank and authority, and so on. These things, being matters of mere administration, they tend not to get told about. Their teachers may not know about them: although the great majority of psychiatrists are going to work in psychiatric hospitals the orientation of their teachers may be exclusively towards matters of analytic psychotherapy, or, more probably, to those respects in which psychiatry, by using psychoactive drugs, can cease to be a matter of human relationships at all. And even where these things are known about nothing may be said. It seems as though in training practitioners for the welfare professions, and in this connection psychiatry may be separated from the rest of medical practice and considered along with teaching and social work, there is an actual resistance to looking at the facts of practice.

Some light is shed on this situation by considering not the welfare professions but those professions that are science-based. Here the Platonic theory of knowledge finds no place. Involvement, contact with practice, is central to the training of the engineer. Even in medicine 'involvement' has been avoided only for the protection of the practitioner. In no science based profession is there any suggestion that insight is blurred by contact with practice. It is conceivable that medicine might be organized on a Platonic basis, that meditation on the nature of Health might be seen as a prerequisite of professional success. Indeed such an approach was distinctive of mediaeval times, and was found in the training of physicians until the nineteenth century.[1] Similarly the dilettante architect is a figure of the only recent past: John Ruskin still found it necessary to distinguish between architects and 'architecturalists'. But such professionals antedate the emergence of distinctive technologies in their respective professions, and one supposes that the Platonic approach could not now succeed for three very good reasons. Taking medicine as the type case these are firstly the emergence of a technology that has to be mastered by the student, the pressing nature of which leaves him progressively less time or inclination to speculate on such matters as the nature of health and disease. One simple

---

[1] 'The select group of English physicians were trained to be first and foremost gentlemen. They were familiar with the writings of Greek and Latin scholars; their medical knowledge was acquired in libraries rather than by contact with the sick. Even when they came to practise they rarely saw any patients. . . . In their efforts to maintain their status and privileges, physicians disdained surgery and pharmacy as mere crafts and trades. No real professional man could allow the brain to be dulled by manual work. . . .' (Holloway, 1964.)

reason for the abstruse nature of much that is taught in departments of education may be simply that there is relatively little to master, (though the need for students to be acquainted with language laboratories and teaching machines may change the content of these courses in the future). The second reason is that with the appearance of definable techniques there appear clear criteria of success or failure in the use of these techniques, a development that tends sooner or later to lead to the observation that the philosophically ignorant may be pragmatically successful. And the third reason emerges from this, that as a profession becomes technical and pragmatic absolute concepts such as Health are found to be notions that one does not in fact use in practice. Only non-practitioners, the very senior and the retired, seem to concern themselves with this at all.[1]

With the appearance of a distinctive technology the tendency seems to be for professional objectives to move from the philosophical to the pragmatic. With this change there appears the possibility of measurable criteria of success or failure, and with this in turn the possibility of manifest excellence or incompetence in practice. A profession undergoing such a development is likely to let go of the Platonic apron strings; the Platonic theory of knowledge and the Platonic structure of power are alike irrelevant. Education and penology on the other hand, having little technology to speak of lack either clear objectives or performance criteria. It may be that this is only as it should be, that dealing with people we ought not to employ a purely instrumental approach (though we have then to explain why we make an exception in the case of doctors). But whatever the reason for it the situation of welfare practice permits the claim for Platonic direction to succeed. Prison staffs and teachers are alike in some doubt about what they are up to and this gives the pure theorist a chance. In fact there are aspects of the job of teacher and borstal housemaster that daily challenge the Platonic assumptions, as we have already seen. But knowledge of this kind rarely rises above the level of know-how, and by and large this know-how

---

[1] Zilboorg states the matter forcibly: 'The medical man, insofar as he seeks knowledge, wants simply to know which are the processes which go on in the human body; insofar as he is a practising healer he is primarily interested in the problem as to which means he can use in order to lead the given life processes to a favourable outcome. There is no need in either case for the concept of illness...' Or, conversely, health. (Zilboorg, 1948.)

tends not to be communicated formally. Neither prison staffs nor teachers seem to be very good at conceptualizing and communicating the realities of their situation.[1] It may be that daily practice is all-absorbing. It may be that there is a general acquiescence to the Platonic situation (one has to remember that graduates are still the minority in both educational and correctional work). It may even be that we lack a vocabulary and conceptual frameworks appropriate to express this kind of knowledge. But whatever the reason the monopoly of comment seems to be in the hands of the non-practitioner.

It is of course a commonplace that in the Platonic scheme, and in social systems based on the Platonic premises, a low value is placed on practice. Any answer to the question of why Platonism survives notwithstanding the onslaughts that in recent years have been made on the Platonic philosophy at a systematic level must stress the desire in all of us to be influential and yet remain gentlemen. In the science-based professions it is possible to do this as a practitioner, for the very presence of a technology, of manifest expertise, secures for the practitioner a virtuoso status that is highly valued. But the business of dealing with children or borstal boys on a day to day basis is quite another matter. It is difficult for anyone whose working life is of this nature to think of himself as in any sense a virtuoso, an expert, or even a professional. It may be, indeed, that on this account the welfare professions tend to attract those who will be content not to be conspicuous and notable in the conduct of affairs. But this only ensures that activities such as penology and education remain the last preserve of the aristocrat and the amateur.

It is now possible to attempt a more searching explanation of

[1] The situation is changing, at least as far as prison and borstal staffs are concerned, with the appearance of a training philosophy that sees the future to lie in continuous education. As practitioners are brought back to the training establishment at frequent intervals throughout their career the importance of the introductory training period diminishes. Similar developments are now taking place in the training of administrative staffs in the hospital service. Such developments inevitably affect the content of training, and modify the traditional relationship between theory and practice. Not only is the training 'course' replaced by the training *conference*, in which the realities of practice are brought to the fore, but the trainer finds himself dealing with experienced practitioners who are not easy to deceive. Such developments seem likely to have a considerable effect on the quality of published comment, and through this on the status of the practitioner. There is no sign, however, of a similar development taking place in the world of education. With the fragmentation of employing authorities this would probably be difficult to accomplish.

the poor relationships that commonly exist in the welfare professions between the practitioner and those who direct his activities. 'Failure of communication' is a phrase that explains nothing, though its popularity is significant for it carries the implication that communication failure is fortuitous, perhaps semantic, certainly nobody's fault, and to be mended by the laying-on of conferences. This, though cosy, serves only to mask the frequency with which communication failures overlie more basic problems about the disposition of power. Thus one might reflect that the relationship between trainer and practitioner is not to be understood until it is appreciated how far training and practice are separate and to some extent mutually opposed careers, that theory and practice are seen as different activities and of different worth. One reason for the uneasy state of the welfare professions is that translation from practitioner to trainer (or administrator) is generally seen as a promotion, while in the science-based professions it is not. The university lecturer in a medical speciality may be earning less than he would have done in full time practice, certainly much less than he would have done in general practice; the university lecturer in education has reached the top of his profession. And the actual business of being a teacher is something that is quickly, perhaps gladly forgotten once the classroom has been left behind: the smell of chalk and children, the daily routines of giving out, taking in, marking and giving out again, the mechanics of registration and dinner-money collection are too quickly replaced by memories of the relatively infrequent occasions when one was conscious of being engaged in that common pursuit of learning that is supposed to be the essence of the educational experience. Likewise the assistant governor seconded to the Prison Service Staff College may find the daily routines of supervising recreation and dealing with staff difficulties falling into the background to be replaced by memories of those occasions when he was engaged in an intimate casework situation, or otherwise involved in treatment, or in whatever the 'real work' is supposed to have been. The assistant governor will inevitably be returned to the world of practice; the lecturer in education almost equally inevitably will not. The problem is at its most acute in education, where the morale of practitioners seems to be particularly low. But the prison official has the civil servant and the social scientist to contend with and is inclined to feel, along with the teacher, that notwithstanding anything they may say to the contrary these are not his colleagues but his masters. Nor does the argument that these are merely functional differences impress. 'It is merely that we have a different job to do' carries little conviction in the face of manifest differences in salary, social status and autonomy.

I am inclined to think, therefore, that the trouble with our welfare professions is political, that it stems from the distinction between gentlemen and players that is so constant a feature of English life. If this is correct it would seem to follow that no real improvement in our educational and correctional services is likely until we are prepared to contemplate quite radical changes in our social life and attitudes; conversely that any real improvement, any genuine professionalism in these areas is likely to bring in its train social changes that not all of us will welcome. One wonders whether there is really as great an anxiety to improve the quality of teachers and prison officials[1] as is commonly claimed. Such a development would put a lot of us out of business. It would also deprive many people of left-ish views of the opportunity to cultivate a moral fastidiousness that is infinitely gratifying. Liberal intellectuals are right to be shocked by the confusion they find in the worlds of education and penal policy, but one suspects that their concern is rather often accompanied by a comfortable sense of being well out of it. Certainly gestures of deference, verbal genuflections, are regularly made in the direction of teachers, probation officers, prison and borstal staffs, mental hospital nurses and others who work in what are recognized to be difficult circumstances. But one constantly catches echoes of a remark of Stendhal's that exactly expresses the attitude of the fashionable liberal: 'I love the people . . . but every moment would be a torture to me if I had to live with the people!' And sometimes the tone is harder, for it is easier to quiet our consciences if we can assure ourselves that those who do these jobs are rather second rate anyway, that the main trouble with educa-

[1] Or the police. There are plenty of indications that a high calibre, thoroughly professional police service would be as unwelcome to the middle class intellectual as to the habitual criminal. The ghost of Lord Peter Wimsey walked as recently as November 1966 when, *a propos* of telephone tapping, the *Guardian* reported the story then doing the rounds of the Left-wing peer who 'got so fed up with clicks and heavy breathing on his phone that he finally snapped, "Oh, for pity's sake, constable, get off the line!" Short pause: "Sorry, sir." Click.'

tion is the teachers, and that we could do the job so much better if we did not have so many more important things to do. This is where aristocracy, liberalism and reform come together, for it is only the aristocrat, who has effectively removed himself from the humdrum world of practice who can afford to be a liberal reformer. No one was more acutely aware of the disdain that so often motivates such people than George Orwell. His essay on Rudyard Kipling is directly on this point:

'But because he identified himself with the official class, he does possess one thing which "enlightened" people seldom or never possess, and that is a sense of responsibility. The middle-class Left hate him for this quite as much as for his cruelty and vulgarity. All Left-wing parties in the highly industrialised countries are at bottom a sham, because they make it their business to fight against something which they do not really wish to destroy. They have internationalist aims, and at the same time they struggle to keep up a standard of life with which those aims are incompatible. We all live by robbing Asiatic coolies, and those of us who are "enlightened" all maintain that those coolies ought to be set free; but our standard of living and hence our "enlightenment" demands that the robbery shall continue. A humanitarian is always a hypocrite, and Kipling's understanding of this is perhaps the central secret of his power to create telling phrases. It would be difficult to hit off the one-eyed pacifism of the English in fewer words than in the phrase, "making mock of uniforms that guard you while you sleep".'

It may be true, as Mr. Vaizey suggests, that hospital sisters, prison 'warders'[1] and others choose their jobs for second rate reasons. The fact remains that at the moment and for the forseeable future these jobs have to be done, and by and large the people who do them probably do them as well as they can. It may be objected that the influence exerted on social policy by vaguely liberal dons and other literati is, after all, very slight. This may be so; nevertheless every fashionable half truth, every facile performance on television or in the weekend supplement by that much lowers the quality of public debate, and this is not what academics, at least, should be doing. And certainly the influence of this kind of behaviour on the *morale* of a profession can be very great indeed. Anyone who has had much to do with teachers and

---

[1] The term has not been used officially since 1922.

correctional workers in particular will know how long it takes to break through the barrier of mistrust that has been created by years of random and ill-informed comment from people who ought to know better. The gap between teachers and educationists, correctional staffs and many criminologists is now sufficiently wide to raise the question whether we have not a crisis of confidence on our hands in these two professions at least.

Nor, again, is it sufficient to describe the situation as a problem in communication. Problems of communication regularly conceal problems about the disposition of power, and the fact of the matter is that in the welfare professions power and responsibility are seldom found together. This is flagrantly the case with welfare planning. Effective planning means consultation with the practitioner, if only to ensure that objectives bear some relation to practical possibility. So the hospital service is beginning to appreciate the importance of having nursing opinion represented in the planning of new hospitals, and the dangers of supposing that either doctors or matrons can speak on their behalf. There are no signs that either the Department of Education and Science or the Home Office have reached this degree of sophistication. Teachers in some local authorities are still required to submit for approval any material they may wish to publish, a procedure that effectively ensures that *a priori* thinking shall never be embarrassed by mere fact, and as these words are written (November 11th, 1966) the *Spectator* carries the startling information that one local authority has warned its teachers against public expression of opposition to that authority's plans for comprehensive education. Similarly anyone who has much to do with the correctional world notices how the poor quality of much penological comment is perpetuated by the Official Secrets Act, and by the dampening effect that civil service procedures have on the urge to answer back. Members of the prison and borstal services do not often publish in the learned journals, but this is not because they have nothing to say. The considerable voice that external bodies have in the discussion of penal and educational policy is due in no small part to the absence of opposition, and one wonders how far we in the universities would really welcome the emergence of an opinion that was both articulate and informed.

Bibliography

ARMFELT, R., *The New Secondary Education*, H.M.S.O. 1947.
ARMYTAGE, W. H G., *Heavens Below. Utopian Experiments in England, 1560-1960.* Routledge and Kegan Paul. 1961.
BALNIEL, LORD, 'The upper class', *Twentieth Century*, Vol. 167, No. 999, May, 1960.
BERNE, E., *Games people play*. André Deutsch. 1966.
BIDERMAN, A. D. and ZIMMER, H. (Eds.), *The Manipulation of Human Behaviour*. Wiley. 1961.
BOTTOMORE, T. B., *Sociology: a Guide to Problems and Literature*. Allen and Unwin. 1962.
BRANTON, N., *The Theory and Practice of Management*. Chatto and Windus. 1960.
BREWSTER SMITH, M., 'Optima of mental health', *Psychiatry*, 13, 503, 1950.
BURNS, E. M., *Ideas in conflict*. Norton. 1960. (Methuen, University Paperbacks, 1963.)
CARR-SAUNDERS, A. and WILSON, P. A., *The Professions*. Oxford University Press. 1933.
COHEN, G., *What's wrong with Hospitals?* Penguin. 1964.
COLLINS, P., *Dickens and Crime*. Macmillan. 1962.
CRAFT, M., 'Psychopathic personalities: a review of diagnosis, aetiology, prognosis and treatment', *B.J. Criminology*, Vol. 1, No. 3, Jan. 1961.
DONNISON, D. V. and CHAPMAN, V., *Social Policy and Administration*. Allen and Unwin. 1965.
DU CANN, R., *The Art of the Advocate*. Penguin. 1964.
ELKIN, W., *The English Penal System*. Penguin. 1957.
ELTON, LORD, *The Revolutionary Idea in France 1789-1871*. Arnold. 1923.
EYSENCK, H. J., *Crime and Personality*. Routledge and Kegan Paul. 1964.
FINDLAY, J. J., *Arnold of Rugby*. Cambridge University Press. 1897.
FOX, L., *The English Prison and Borstal System*. Routledge and Kegan Paul. 1952.
GIBBENS, T. C. N., Recent trends in the management of psychopathic offenders', *B.J. Delinquency*, Vol. 2, p. 103, 1951.
GOULDNER, A. W., 'Explorations in Applied Social Science', *Social problems*, III (3), 1956.

Bibliography

GRAHAM, N. W., 'Planning procedures', in Bell (Ed.), *Hospital and Medical School Design*. Livingstone. 1962.

HAMMOND, J. L. and B., *The Bleak Age*. Penguin. 1947.

H.M.S.O., *The Organisation of After-care: Report of the Advisory Council on the Treatment of Offenders*. 1963.

HOLLOWAY, S. W. F., 'Medical education in England', *History*, Vol. XLIX, No. 167, October 1964.

HOWARD, D. L., *The English Prisons*. Methuen. 1960.

HUMBLE, J. W., *Improving Management Performance*. British Institute of Management. 1965.

JONES, H., *Crime and the Penal System*. University Tutorial Press Ltd., second edition. 1962.

JONES, K., *Lunacy, Law and Conscience, 1744-1845*. Routledge and Kegan Paul. 1955.

JONES, K., 'Mental Hospitals: Evaluation', *New Society*, December 6th, 1962.

JONES, K. and SIDEBOTHAM, R., *Mental Hospitals at Work*. Routledge and Kegan Paul. 1962.

LUSTIBERG, V., 'Sleep Learning', *New Education*, March 1965.

MCGREGOR, O. R., 'Social Facts and the Social Conscience', *Twentieth Century*, May 1966.

MACIVER, R., *Society, a Textbook of Sociology*. Macmillan. 1937.

MERTON, R. K., *Social Theory and Social Structure*. Free Press. 1957.

MORRIS, T. and P., *Pentonville: a Sociological Study of an English Prison*. Routledge and Kegan Paul. 1963.

NOKES, P., 'Planning and the Prison Service', *B.J. Criminology*, Vol. 7, No. 3, 1967.

ORWELL, GEORGE, 'Rudyard Kipling', in *Critical Essays*, 1946.

PACKARD, V., *The Hidden Persuaders*. Longmans. 1957.

PETERS, R. S., *Authority and Responsibility in Education*. Allen and Unwin. 1959.

RAPOPORT, R. N., 'Oscillations and sociotherapy', *Human Relations*, Vol. IX, No. 3, 1956.

RAPOPORT, R. N., *Community as doctor*. Tavistock Publications. 1960.

RICE, K., *Productivity and Social Organisation: the Ahmedabad Experiment*. Tavistock Publications. 1958.

RICE, K., *The Enterprise and its Environment*. Tavistock Publications. 1963.

ROBERTSON, J., *Young Children in Hospital*. Tavistock Publications. 1958.

SIMON, H. A., *Administrative Behaviour: a study of Decision-making processes in Administrative Organisation*. Free Press. 1945.

SPOLTON, L., 'The Secondary School in Post-war Fiction, *B.J. Educational Studies*, Vol. XI. 1963.

Bibliography

STAFFORD-CLARK, D., *Psychiatry Today*. Penguin. 1952.

STANTON, A. H. and SCHWARTZ, M., *The Mental Hospital*. Basic Books. 1954.

STOKES, SEWELL, Review of H. J. Klare, 'Anatomy of Prison', *Prison Service Journal*, Vol. 1, No. 1, July 1960.

SULLIVAN, H. S., *The Psychiatric Interview*. Norton. 1954.

TAYLOR, W., *The Secondary Modern School*. Faber. 1963.

TIDMARSH, et al., *Capital punishment: the case for abolition*. Sheed and Ward. 1963.

VAIZEY, J., *Scenes from Institutional Life*. Faber. 1959.

VAIZEY, J., *Britain in the Sixties: Education for Tomorrow*. Penguin. 1962.

VAIZEY, J., *The Economics of Education*. Faber. 1962.

VAIZEY, J., *The Control of Education*. Faber. 1963.

VOELCKER, P. M. W., 'Juvenile courts: the parents' point of view', *B.J. Criminology*, Vol. 1, 154, 1960.

VOLD, G. B., *Theoretical Criminology*. Oxford University Press. 1958.

VON NEUMANN, J. and MORGENSTERN, O., *Theory of Games and Economic Behaviour*. Princeton University Press, 1947.

WALKER, N., *Crime and Punishment in Britain*. Edinburgh University Press. 1965.

WEBER, M., *The Sociology of Religion*. Methuen. 1965.

WHYTE, W. H., *The Organisation Man*. Jonathan Cape. 1957.

WILENSKY, H. L., 'The Dynamics of Professionalism: the Case of Hospital Administration', *Hospital Administration*, Vol. 7, No. 2, Spring 1962.

WILKINS, L. T., 'Criminology: an operational research approach', in Welford, A. T., et al, *Society: problems and methods of study*. Routledge and Kegan Paul. 1962.

WOODHAM-SMITH, C., *Florence Nightingale*. Collins. 1951.

WYMER, N., *Dr. Arnold of Rugby*. Robert Hale. 1953.

ZILBOORG, G., 'The Struggle for and against the Individual in Psychotherapy', *Am. J. Psychiatry*, 104, No. 8, 1948.

Index

Index

Index

Mannheim, Karl, 65
Marx, Karl, 77
Mathematics, 118
Medical profession, 7-9, 33, 84, 94, 109, 111-12, 114, 122, 127
Medical social workers, 15
Medication, 90, 94, 99, 108
Medicine, vii, 42-4, 46, 52, 70-2 77, 87, 89-95, 101, 106, 121, 124
Mental Hospitals: see Psychiatric Hospitals
Mental Welfare Officers, 15
Merton, R. K., 39, 45
Mesmerism, 53
Ministry of Health, xi, 111
Mill, James, 48
Misunderstanding, 57
Monitorial system, 36
Morale, 8-11, 26-8, 32, 126
Morality, 23, 41, 43, 45, 52, 63, 65, 72, 76, 78, 80-6, 88, 102
Morgenstern, O., 20
Morris, P., 68
Morris, T., 68, 85, 100

National Association of School-masters, 52
National Union of Teachers, 26-27, 51-2
Natural Crime, 76, 78
Natural Law, 79
Negotiation, 32
New Secondary Education, 3, 61
New Society, 40, 88, 99
Nightingale, Florence, 23
Nokes, P., 4
Normality, 41
Norman, Frank, 61-2
Norwich scheme, 6
Novels, 35, 51
Nurses, Nursing profession, xi, 5-6, 23-4, 28, 43, 92-3, 99, 115-16, 125-7
Nursing procedures, xi, 5-6, 24

Objectives, 1-16, 20, 22, 24-33, 34, 39-40, 43-5, 48, 53-8, 60-1, 71, 73, 75, 83, 85, 87, 97, 111, 119, 122, 127
Objectivity, 64-5, 77, 86
Occupational therapy, 91
Official Secrets Act, 127
Operational research, 29, 38, 71, 80
Operations (surgical), 91-3
Organisational setting of activity, 28, 68, 100-1, 119
Orwell, George, 38, 126
Outcomes, 21-2
Outpatient departments, 99
Oxford Group, 104

Packard, Vance, 41
Pangloss, Dr., 53
Pareto, V., 86
Parkinson, Professor C. N., 35
Pastoral professions, x-xi
Paterson, Sir A., 16, 37
Patients, 89-95, 103-4, 106-7, 109-110
Pay-off: see also Manifest, Disaster Criteria, 20
Penal Administration: see Correctional work
Penal Policy, 40, 43, 47, 54, 57, 71, 73, 78, 80, 82, 85, 112-13
Penology: see Penal Policy, Correctional work
Pennsylvania Regime, 47
Pentonville System, 47-8, 57, 68
Performance Criteria, 10, 15, 21, 63, 102, 122
Permissiveness, 110
Personal experience, 104-5
Personal qualities, 34-7
Peters, R. S., 28, 30
Philanthropic activity, 42, 52-3, 57
Philosophy, 72, 76-8, 80, 84, 117

137

Index

Residual category, 61
Resocialisation, 37, 42, 44
Resources, 43, 53, 87, 92
Responsibility, 19, 100, 109, 127
Retreat, York, 24
Retribution, 78–85
Rice, K., 1, 13
Ritualism, 10–11
Robertson, J., 5
Role, 69, 74, 78
Rousseau, Jean-Jacques, 66
Rush, Benjamin, 53
Ruskin, John, 121

Sacramental acts, qualities, 23–4, 34, 37
Salaries, 26–7, 115, 125
Salmon Committee Report, 1966, xi
Saltpetriere hospital, 53, 103
Schools, 3, 7–8, 10–11, 13–14, 16, 24, 30–31, 44, 49–52, 58, 60–61, 67, 89, 94–5, 101–2, 106–107, 110, 115–16, 118–20
Schwartz, M., 31, 99
Science, 40–41, 52, 65–6, 69, 71, 74, 78–87, 102, 121, 123
'Secondary modern shocker', 51–52
Security (prisons), xi, 12
Semantics, 76–8, 124
Sensibility, 65
Sensitivity training, 107
Sex Offenders, 37
Shaftsbury, Lord, 60
Shaw, Bernard, 25
Shroud-waving, 7
Sidebotham, R., 14
Simon, H. A., 29
Sixth-forms, 58–9
Skills, 2, 19, 24, 34–45, 95, 97, 101, 106, 111–12
Sleep-learning, 38, 40, 102
Smith, Adam, 40

Social casework, viii, 19, 35–6, 40, 42, 60, 80, 97–9, 101–2, 114, 124
Social change, 1, 14–15, 107–8, 125
Social conflict theory of criminality 77
Social control, 109–110
Social distance, ix, 18–19, 37, 88, 95, 102
Social engineering, 23
Social order, 82, 109–110
Social policy, 63, 77, 82, 86–7, 126
Social problems, 52, 57, 69
Social relationships, ix–xi, 34, 36–7, 41–2, 86–8, 89, 91–5, 99–100, 105, 110, 115
Social science, 49, 63–88, 124
Social work, vii, 26, 97–9, 109, 114, 118, 121
Sociology, 17–18, 40, 63, 65–6, 70, 72, 74, 78, 82–8, 89, 107, 118
Sociology of knowledge, 65–6
Sophists, 41
Space, 89–91, 94–5, 97
Spectator, 52, 127
Spiritual osmosis, 36
Spolton, L., 52
Spontaneity, 34–5, 42, 93, 109–10
Sport, 38–9
Sprott, W. J. H., 40, 77
Stafford-Clark, D., 46, 52–4
Standardisation (of treatment), 107–8
Stanton, A., 31, 99
'Staff sociologist', 70–1, 74
Stendhal, 125
Stokes, Sewell, 112
Students, x, 1–2, 14–15, 24–5, 35, 59
Sullivan, H. S., 31, 35
'Superannuation' (in Arnold's system), 59
Surgery, Surgeons, vii, 19, 21, 25, 37, 90–5, 99, 101, 107–8

139

For Product Safety Concerns and Information please contact our EU
representative GPSR@taylorandfrancis.com
Taylor & Francis Verlag GmbH, Kaufingerstraße 24, 80331 München, Germany

www.ingramcontent.com/pod-product-compliance
Lightning Source LLC
Chambersburg PA
CBHW050529270326
41926CB00015B/3140

9 780415 863759